A PROVEN STEP-BY-STEP SYSTEM TO OWNING YOUR FUTURE

BREAK FREE ENTREPRENEUR

How to Safely and Smartly Make the Leap to Self-Employment

ANDY GARRISON, MBA, CFP®

ISBN: 978-1-7377739-2-4 (paperback)

Printed in the United States of America.

DON'T MISS THESE FREE TOOLS!

BreakFreeMoneyBook.com/Resources

Here you will get free access to several worksheets and "extras" to help you safely and smartly make the move to self-employment!

You'll also have the opportunity to join our free community for support and even win some one-on-one coaching to help you break free!

BreakFreeMoneyBook.com/Resources

THIS BOOK IS A TEACHING TOOL - NOT ADVICE

This book is a teaching tool and is for educational purposes only. The views expressed in it are mine alone and nothing should be considered financial, legal, or tax advice.

While I put everything I know to work for me and many others in this book, I can't guarantee you (or anyone) specific results from reading this (or any book). Because of that, neither myself nor the publisher accepts any liability in any form as a result of this book.

Now that I've shared that, know this: I have faith in you! I believe you can do whatever you put your mind to, including successfully breaking free!

CONTENTS

Part 2
Getting Your Financial House In Order And Establishing Your "Financial Runway"

Part 3
Putting It All Together In A Plan And Taking Action

A QUICK NOTE: HOW TO USE THIS BOOK

This book is made up of three main sections.

The first part (Chapter 2 through Chapter 7) is designed to help you identify exactly what you can uniquely do to succeed in business on your own. If you don't know what you should do to break free to self-employment, this was built for you.

The second part (Chapter 8 through Chapter 10) helps you get a grasp on your current financial position and shares how to prepare yourself financially for the move to self-employment. If you have family obligations, are the breadwinner, or are more conservative by nature, you'll appreciate this section.

The third and final part (Chapter 11 and Chapter 12) shows you how to put it all together into a working plan that keeps you on track and how to battle some of the fear and doubt that might creep in on your journey. If you're unsure of how to put everything together in a workable way that accomplishes your goals or are worried about what might go wrong, dive into this part.

While I believe most people would benefit from reading the book in order, from start to finish, you can start at whatever section you feel is most appropriate. If you skip around, I would encourage you to at least "breeze through" the chapters you feel you have a lock on. There's always something we can find that can better our odds, so don't let it pass you by when you have it at your fingertips!

However you use this book (or the resources referenced throughout), know that I'm cheering for you and can't wait to welcome you to the "other side" of employment. The grass really is greener!

FOREWORD

YOU MUST *OWN* YOUR INCOME TO CONTROL YOUR FUTURE.

I've known Andy Garrison for a number of years. We met through a nonprofit we both support and it quickly became obvious we had a lot in common. Most importantly our priorities of "faith first, family second, and finances third" were aligned.

Even though we had different gifts, we shared a desire to positively impact others. We both felt led to help others become all they dreamt of becoming. I had made a career of doing exactly that, and after an eight-hour road trip together, my instincts told me Andy was going to do the same. But Andy had the potential to do it in a bigger and broader way. Andy just needed to "break free" first.

Andy was a financial advisor with a wealth management firm. I had spent over 30 years developing thousands of successful leaders and hundreds of multi-millionaires in that same industry. Andy was primarily focused on the top 5% of income earners and I worked primarily with the other 95% of people in North America. But the financial (and business) principles were the same.

Andy has become an incredible teacher. It is a gift around which he has developed a special skill set. One thing that makes Andy such a great teacher (trust me...if you invest the time to read this book, you'll know Andy is a great teacher) is he is first of all a great student.

He understands that the best students are many times the best teachers. He learns with a purpose. He knows he will likely be teaching what he learns. He feels called to help others learn and benefit from what he has learned. He stores the lessons away in his brain, with the purpose of using them to teach others in the future.

Andy's integrity has him stick to what he knows. He wants to make sure he masters a subject as a student before he begins to teach it to others. He doesn't try to teach something that he hasn't already learned AND APPLIED in his own life. That's why this book, and I believe many written in the future, will be so impactful.

He is great at organizing good ideas into a simple to understand format. How do I know that? Because after he "picked my brain" for eight hours he said "Shane, you have to write a book!" I said, "Yeah, I have about 20 very impactful books started but I'm a much better speaker, leader, and motivator than a writer." He said, "I'll help you."

Helping other successful people get their brains downloaded to written form is one of Andy's gifts. I learned through the process of writing a #1 best seller (*God Wants YOU to Win!*) together that Andy has a way to simplify things. His GIFT is to communicate A LOT of important information into a few simple words. He is incredibly efficient with words. No fluff, just ideas simplified with the fewest words possible.

Before we spent that original eight hours together, Andy had been in the financial advisory industry for 13 years and had helped clients accumulate about $35 million of combined AUM (assets under management) after many stops and starts. He wanted to do more.

He applied what he learned in that eight hours and less than a year later he had accumulated nearly $130 million of AUM. Then around $230 million AUM. The problem was he was a W-2 employee. He owned *nothing*, not even control over his future.

I had gotten to know his young family very well. I cared about them like family. To be honest, I think everyone in Andy's life feels like family. If you interviewed his clients they would tell you he is easy to get along with and they get that "family feel" as well.

I knew it was only a matter of time before everything he had built for the corporation he worked for and clients he had developed would be taken from him. It's just how the system is set up.

Andy had spent over 15 years working very hard, doing the right thing, helping others get what they wanted, and had become a top earner. He was in the top 1% of earners in the United States of America, in fact. At that point, a company usually no longer needs that person. Not a highly compensated one anyway.

The person that had built millions in revenue for the firm has served his purpose. The hard work has been done, and the company would soon find a way to eliminate that W-2 employee. They replace them with someone not nearly as good, but also not nearly as highly compensated. They didn't need to bring in the clients. They just needed to service the clients.

He had done everything asked of him and more. He went above and beyond to build an incredible value for the company he worked for. Yet he owned nothing! It could all be taken from him in an instant. And it wasn't a matter of IF - it was only a matter of when. It might be taken away a little bit at a time or all at once, but W-2 employees ALWAYS HAVE IT TAKEN AWAY one way or another.

I didn't want that for him and his wonderful family, so I started encouraging him to find a better way. I told him he needed to prepare to become the owner of his life. Owner of his own business. It was time to start putting things in place to make his own family's dreams come true. He could stay focused on helping his clients' dreams come true, but he had to move toward independent contractor status and develop ownership for himself and his family.

Andy did just that! AND he documented *everything* he learned from the process so he could teach others to do the same thing. If you're holding this book in your hands, you're a very lucky individual. Andy has simplified the process for you. I encourage you to follow the steps he lays out so you can start to own your life and own YOUR business.

I consider it an honor to write the foreword to this book. If you've made it to this point, I've already said a prayer for you. I pray you gain tremendous clarity through the process in this book. I pray it gives you the confidence you need to follow through on the dreams God has placed in your heart. I truly believe your dreams are a gift from God, and what you do with them is your gift back! Andy gives you the step by step process to FINALLY BREAK FREE.

If you've been praying for clarity...HERE'S YOUR SIGN!

Break Free,
Shane Rudman

PREFACE

This Can Work For You!

We've all been "here." Tired and burned out from building someone else's dream, pouring in all the extra hours at a cost to our own dreams and family. That's been acceptable, though, because we've been paid well for our time. We've been able to take care of our family. But now, it's different.

Now, you're ready to hit the next level and become a successful entrepreneur. You're ready to leverage the skills you have built over the years to create your own freedom and do something great for yourself and your family.

It's exhilarating and scary at the same time. You *know* deep down you have what it takes, but you also don't want to make a mistake and risk what you've accomplished, saved for, and built with your family so far. I hear you!

Let me tell you this, though: no matter where you are in life right now, you *can* break free from your job and start your own business safely and smartly, *even if* you have a family and massive obligations. I felt the same way, and I know many others that have too. I made the leap and haven't looked back.

This book lays out all of the steps needed to safely and successfully "break free" while maintaining your family obligations. It's a well-thought-out process that will help you build the certainty you need to make the leap and take control of your future.

It worked for me and I know it'll work for you, too!

➤ Making The Leap

I always had dreams of "doing my own thing" and running my own business but for the longest time, I never took the leap and did it. I contented myself with being stuck as a cog in the wheel for someone else for all the reasons we all do. It's "safe." It's comfortable. Until those days when it's not come along.

Probably like you, I've had many moments where "this was it," "I'm definitely doing it," and "I'm breaking out on my own," but the problem was I never actually did anything about it. I had a long list of false starts. I didn't realize it at the time, but it was because I was always missing either the *motivation* to do it or the *how-to* to do it.

The motivation came around when the COVID-19 pandemic worked its way through the corporate world. It wasn't so much the pandemic as it was realizing how much the company I was working for had control over my life, and what I was giving up to serve the organization.

On paper, things were great. I was earning over $500k a year and doing great work with clients I loved with a great team. But something wasn't right. I was constantly stressed and was rarely present with my family.

I finally realized that I was for sale. The time with my kids was for sale - even the day my son was born, I was doing work for someone else's business. The time to build my own dreams was for sale. *Every aspect of my life was for sale, including my joy, simply to build someone else's perfect life.*

Then it hit me: Why couldn't I do that for myself?

The problem was, I was absolutely terrified of "doing my own thing."

How would I make money?

What about health insurance?

Will I have credibility?

Will I let my family down?

Will I lose my identity as a "successful" employee?

Those questions held me back until I realized it was just *fear*. Fear of failing and all that goes along with it. But fear can be managed and conquered.

I made a decision to act, in spite of that fear, and I went about making a *plan*. Maybe you're in the same spot now - ready to break free and start your own business but you know you won't jump without a *plan*. As you'll learn, a plan is the tangible "playbook" that gives you everything you need to be certain you're going to be successful *before* you make the move.

I knew enough about myself to know I wouldn't make the jump if I didn't have a plan in place. More times than I could count, I would come up with a great idea, get really excited, and then get "stuck" because I didn't lay out a path to make it a reality.

Then it hit me that I needed to combine my two skill sets and specialities and "practice what I'd been preaching." Every day I help successful people do two things: (1) make financial plans to manage their money and create a legacy, and (2) leverage their expertise to become an authority in their own space.

I knew that if I brought the financial planning together with the "what in the world do I do to create my own freedom" angle, I could build an effective plan to break free. That's what I did and now my only regret is that I didn't do it sooner.

Since that time, I've helped others break free using their expertise to create their own businesses. That has let them experience the same freedom as *millions* of other entrepreneurs that have gone before.

I know you can do it, too! *You have everything you need to be successful creating your own business.* I promise you that, and in this book I'll show you why that's true. You just need a working *plan* to get you there!

My goal for this book is to give you that *plan*. The *plan* is the key and what was missing for me for a long time. The *plan* is your roadmap to being your own boss, to truly controlling your own life. If you follow this process, I believe you're about to cross into the amazing realm of self-employment and build *your* dream!

Are you ready?

INTRODUCTION

The Key To Making It Work

How many times have you seen, read stories, or learned about someone who had made the leap from being an employee to being self-employed and got that "I want it too" feeling in your stomach?

I think it all starts with a big dream of "being our own boss," but for most of us, it goes deeper than that because nothing happens until we really start to want something so much it completely consumes us.

When the constant guilt and discomfort of sacrificing *everything* from your time, family, and joy to serve someone else, to build his or her dream and create freedom for another family, is too much.

Usually, that person isn't "bad" by any means. Most of the time our bosses and employers are good people who already took the leap to believe in themselves and build their own dream. Not always, but most of the time.

We know we deliver more value than we're being paid, especially as salespeople, execs, and consultants (or anyone that is in the path of revenue). Otherwise, the business doesn't work. Because of this, we rationalize what we're doing and try to make sense of it.

For a while, it feels right (or at least we let it feel like it feels right). All we have to do is show up, deliver, and then we get paid - and are usually off a couple of days a week and maybe a few holidays. Except we keep pushing and rarely have a "real" day off. (*Especially* now in the day and age of email and texting at all hours).

That's because we're achievers, though. Most people who make the move from employee to self-employed are. And *all* of the ones who are successful are.

Why?

I believe it's because it's in our nature to go and build something and win. We've seen too many cases of success to *not* believe it's possible for us. But then we face a big problem.

Every time we get the idea or the urge to make the change, something holds us back. Something stops us, and we don't do anything about it.

Each time we do that, it sets us back a little further. We lose faith in ourselves and can spiral down emotionally. Maybe you've been there before - I know I have. Many times.

But I realized something, and I want you to realize it too: it's not that we aren't capable of succeeding, it's just that we never *built a real* plan *to be successful!*

I know that may sound too simplistic, so let me explain. Most people decide on WHAT they want to do ("I want to start my own thing"), but they don't ever decide on HOW they want to do it ("and here's how I'm going to do it").

What's missing isn't just the "how to," but the actual PLAN and the daily ACTIONS, listed out, to get them there with certainty.

I call these REAL plans, not something fluffy or feel-good. They essentially become a roadmap that:

- Gets your financial house in order quickly (allowing you to safely make the leap)
- Identifies your valuable skill(s) and "area of authority" (*the* space where you can be *the* person)
- Helps you become *the* expert for your ideal clients (so they are easy to attract and are sold on you *before* you walk in the room)
- Lays out strategies to generate sufficient new business (making sure your leap really does pay off in the end)
- Gives you a *simple* but *effective* plan to get it all done (so you don't struggle to take action)
- Is dynamic and *adapts* along the way with you (ensuring you never get stuck)

In other words, it's a playbook that gives you the answers to all of the "what ifs," including the low-probability-but-big-impact events like dealing with economic upheavals, the struggle of getting clients, changing regulations, and just plain bad luck. Having this gives you the confidence and tactics to move forward and successfully start your own business.

Just as I mentioned before, I don't have all the answers, but I've always discovered ways to find out what I don't know. Likewise, I didn't create all of the techniques needed to be successful, but I have learned how to leverage them in my journey and know you can, too.

So that leaves us with my promise to you. If you read this and go through the steps, you *will* have the playbook that allows you to say, "See ya!" to a life of working away for someone else's dream and, instead, going and building your own.

CHAPTER

1

Following A Proven Process Is What Brings Success

Stories of entrepreneurs starting their successful businesses by "winging it" seem to dominate movies and discussions, but there's a far larger group who have built successful enterprises in a much more consistent and repeatable way.

This group of people knows that *those with a plan do better than those without a plan.* I believe that's true in all areas of life, and it's especially true when we're talking about money and launching a new business.

Sure, planning may not be the most exciting thing one can do, but that doesn't mean it doesn't work! For most of us, we were never taught how to plan effectively in school, life, or business, and that's where the problem starts.

Based on my experiences working with a variety of individuals, very few people have put together a *real* plan. If you count yourself among that group, don't worry, because we're going to break it all down.

But first, what is a *real* plan?

A real plan is a map that gets you from "Point A" to "Point B," taking into account obstacles along the way. It's a playbook that gives you the daily actions to take that move you toward your goal, and ultimately to the success for which you're looking.

More succinctly, it is *a series of small, daily actions that are prioritized and sequenced in a way that delivers a tangible desired outcome.*

There is *zero* vagueness in a real plan. Everything is spelled out and thought through so that you have the confidence it'll work *and* so you know what small accomplishments each day will get you to your goal.

Creating a real plan to successfully build a business and transition to self-employment isn't difficult, but it does take work. That work may be the most effective and profitable thing you do to break free, though, and this process will help you do it smoothly.

➢ The Plan You Will Build

Building your "break free plan" consists of five big steps and having the correct mindset. The book is designed around these steps, starting off with designing the perfect business for *you* and helping you decide *exactly what you can uniquely do* to replace your income through self-employment. Here's a quick breakdown of what you'll pick up:

One - Take Inventory

First, you will take inventory of where you are now, including:

1. Your skills - so you are confident and clear on what you're most qualified to do at the highest level
2. Your reasons - so you are clear on what's driving you away from employment and into self-employment, and most importantly, what you want to have accomplished when you're done
3. Your financial position - so you know where you stand and what needs to be done to provide sufficient "runway" and safety for your transition

A business coach of mine always says, "All progress starts by telling the truth[1]." That means we'll start by getting clear on where you are now so that when it comes time to improve your financial position, design your ideal business, and actually break free, you're ready to go on "day one."

Questions you'll get answers to as we start off include:

- How do I go about taking inventory of my financial life, skills, and motivation?
- How do I know where I stand financially before I make the jump?
- How do I know how much I need to live the life I want?
- What skills should I be taking inventory of?
- What do I do if I don't think my skills are "unique" enough to successfully launch my business? (Hint, they are!)

---

1 I first heard this from Coach Micheal Burt through his Monster Producers program

After answering these questions, you're ready to go to work and start reaping the rewards of your planning.

Two - Design The Best Business For YOU

When I created my first business to break away from being an employee, I made a mistake that I see a lot of eventually-successful entrepreneurs make: *designing a business that runs you instead of fueling the life you really want.*

This section will help you design a business that will give you the life you want so you end up happy and not frustrated. We'll also walk through how to make sure your transition has the best chance of success, based on your unique combination of experience, knowledge, and skill set.

This part of the process helps you best understand:

- How do I use skills I already have to create revenue right away?
- How do I choose what style of business to pursue?
- Are the choices I have for my business design valuable to the marketplace?
- How do I know who my audience is and who should I market to?
- How can I tell what my audience/market needs?
- What if I don't think I have anything special that no one else has?
- How do I build an offer that people want?
- Where do I get revenue from?
- How do I get access to partners, centers of influence, and my market?
- How can I know if it'll work "fast enough" to be viable?

- How will I know if I'm actually able to do all of this?
- Can I really design something that covers all the bases and makes for perfect days (and even a perfect life)?

As you finish these tasks, you'll have a solid idea of what type of business/service structure you should build, and then, next, you'll go and build it.

Three - Build (And Enhance) Your Financial Foundation (Your "Runway")

While you're putting all of that together, you want to enhance what I call your financial "runway."

Your financial runway is the amount of time, measured in months, that you can cover your expenses with your current assets and other earnings as you step away from your employment income.

No matter where you are now, there are several things you can do to increase your financial runway. Combined with the techniques you'll use to aim for revenue coming in immediately as you launch, your risk of switching to self-employed is greatly reduced with a longer "runway."

As we go through this part, you'll walk away knowing answers to:

- What exactly is my "financial runway," and what does it mean in relation to moving to self-employed?
- Do I really have options to increase my runway in the timeframe I'm looking at? (And what should I do to do that?)
- What should I do if I'm not in the financial shape I want to be?
- Should I start setting up all of the business stuff right away? (LLCs, bank accounts, website, business cards, etc.)

The best part about working on your "financial runway" is that it will benefit you *after* you launch your business, too. It helps improve your foundation as you break free *and* for the rest of your life.

Four - Formalize Your Business

Once you know the business structure that will best support your life and what you want to do, it's time to create it and bring it to fruition.

The key here is, while staying in the confines of the design you created in step two, to make sure what you build is what your *market* wants and is willing to pay for.

In addition to nailing down your "authority position," or what you can be *the* person in your space for, you'll answer the following questions:

- What "formal" and legal items for my business should I be establishing?
- What do I need to do to cover things like taxes and expenses?
- When should I consider taking money out of my business?
- What are the best tools and resources to run the business effectively?

As you create your business and answer the above questions, you'll be ready to put it all together in a real plan and playbook that helps you *safely* reach self-employment and, ultimately, be in control of your destiny.

Five - Create And Execute Your Plan

Once you have all of the "whats" and "whys" of breaking free from employment and launching your self-employed business, you're ready to plan and execute. This section dives into the "hows" of creating your plan and playbook for success.

You'll lock everything down into a series of actions that are prioritized and sequenced in a way that delivers a tangible desired outcome: a successful launch to self-employment!

You'll take that plan - those series of prioritized and sequenced actions - and schedule your tasks so that you know what you'll do and when, giving you everything you need to get from "Point A" to "Point B."

We'll also walk through a few questions that will give you additional "know how" as you build your plan:

- Is planning really valuable?
- How do I prioritize and sequence the actions I list out?
- Do plans really work?
- How can I make sure my plan works for me?
- How can I build a plan if I've never done it before?

You will be left with a solid plan designed to get you to your goal and launch into self-employment with far less risk to your future and family.

Finally, you'll address one thing that catches even the best entrepreneurs: doubt and "reality" setting in.

Wrap-Up - What Happens Now?

There's no feeling like the "I have it all set and now all I have to do is say 'go!'" feeling when you've planned, tested, and prepared every step for your launch.

Despite having everything in place, fear, masquerading as doubt and perceived "reality," can set in and cause us to question whether or not the transition is really the right thing to do. We can even start telling ourselves that it's not actually *that* bad where we're at now and we can always "try it later."

Even though we *know* inside that launching and pressing "go" is the right thing to do, other people (and even our own minds) can make us doubt ourselves. It happens to *every* entrepreneur and is part of the process. This section will help you get past all of that and take the next step into your future.

This step will help you think through:

- What do I do if I start to doubt myself or feel like I might fail?
- How do I handle it when others say I'm crazy?
- What will I feel as I get started and make the leap?
- How can I guarantee that I take action?
- Are there others like me, feeling the same thing, in the same spot, that can help? (And where do I find them?)

If you're going to go through all of the work, make sure your launch is successful by working through all those self-doubt issues and allows you to take charge of your life.

Now, it's time to dive into breaking free safely, smartly, and with a plan!

PART 1

Design The Right Business And Determine What You Could (And Should) Uniquely Do To Succeed

CHAPTER

2

Your Skills Inventory: Getting Clear On Your Most Valuable Skills And What You Bring To The Table

Your first step in breaking free and starting your own successful business is identifying your most valuable skills. If you know what you're good at and what the marketplace will value, you can better design your business and offer. This puts you in a *much* better financial position right out of the gate and should allow you to replace your income even sooner.

Before you begin, remember: *you have everything you need to make it happen!* If you've ever been paid for work before, then you *know* you have value and can create your own income. Don't worry about having it all figured out - we'll get to that.

For now, your current skills *are* enough to get you to where you want to be and replace your income. This chapter will help you identify and "inventory" your skills so you know exactly what you have and can use to break free successfully.

A note of caution for this section: If you tend to be more reserved when talking about your accomplishments and skills, this step may be challenging at first because it causes you to "brag" a bit about yourself and your capabilities. Don't worry, though, it'll be worth it! Follow along and you'll be glad you did this.

➢ Identifying Your Valuable Skills

The word "skills" tends to have a broad and sometimes vague connotation attached to it. While it's true that nearly anything can be classified as a skill, in this section you will narrow down the skill(s) that the market might value *and* that can generate income for you on "day one" as a self-employed individual.

What Skills Should You Focus On?

Given the broad nature of "skills," which ones should you focus on as you prepare to build your new business? The ones that *are currently most valuable to the marketplace you'll serve.*

Don't worry if you're at a loss for what those are right now. We'll narrow down your skills and help you select the best one for the right market together in upcoming chapters. For now, the focus is on understanding the skills that are somewhat unique to you and provide value to others.

Your Skills Inventory

Now, it's time to start forming your inventory of the things that you're good at doing, making, etc. To begin, list out everything you can think of that you do well, whether it be personal or business. Examples could include selling, negotiating, writing, graphic design work, speaking, teaching, sewing, organization, good with numbers, etc. Don't overthink this part; simply make an inventory of everything that could fit.

As you make your list, it is OK to have some skills on there that you know probably won't fit the bill later in terms of usefulness to the business world. Those can always be removed. If you think you have a skill, list it out now, either with pen and paper or on a spreadsheet.

Once you've listed out everything you can think of, go through the questions below to begin the "adding and refining" process.

Question One - What Is Your Current "Primary Skill?"

Your primary skill is what you spend most of your time doing now, and you likely do it well. It may even be the core focus of your current role. Just know that it isn't the same thing as a job title. A title describes the position you were hired for, a skill explains the core function you do. For example:

- If you're an accountant, your primary skill might be understanding and crunching numbers for businesses (or individuals if you're a CPA)
- If you're a salesperson, your primary skill might be getting deals across the finish line (or communication, or negotiation, etc.)

- If you're a graphic designer, your primary skill might be creating branding or designs that catch the eye of onlookers
- If you're a financial planner, your primary skill might be helping people gain clarity in their financial life
- If you're an engineer, your primary skill might be keeping projects on track and calculating safety tolerances

Don't worry about making this sound enticing or attractive at this point, we'll get to that in a later chapter. I've found that if you are struggling to find your primary skill, it's probably because you're trying too hard or putting too much pressure on yourself. This should be straightforward: take a look at what you do most often and that you do well, and that's your answer.

Take some comfort in knowing two things: (1) whatever your primary skill is, it is valuable (that's why people pay you for it), and (2) if it's something you don't necessarily enjoy and that's why you're wanting to break free, there is a solution. Chapter 4 will help you build a business you love while still leveraging the skills you have now.

Question Two - Ask Others What Talents They Notice

When we are truly good at something, it's likely that it either comes somewhat naturally to us or we've worked so hard at it that it feels second nature when we do it. Because of that, we don't always recognize our "genius" and skills as easily as others see them in us. This means one of the best ways to find out your gifts is to ask other people what they already see in you.

Find four or five people that you know and trust, who would be honest and direct with you, and ask them a simple question. *"If you could choose one or two things that you feel I'm best at, what would they be?"*

For some, that can be uncomfortable, and if that's you or the person you're asking, that's OK. Feel free to give them some time after you ask and say something like, "I know it's catching you off guard a bit, so if it's easier to send a quick text or email later, that's great, too."

This exercise, asking others what they see in you, has proven to be one of the best "eye openers" for people with whom I've had the privilege of walking through this process over the last several years. As John Maxwell says, "It's hard to see the picture when you're inside the frame." In other words, those on the outside can see into us better than we can see ourselves sometimes. You may be surprised to hear what others have to say!

As you go out and ask people, a gentle word of caution is in order. *Sometimes* people forget to get back to you. And sometimes people "hem and haw" a bit while they're thinking, especially if they are caught off guard.

Do *not* read into this and think they can't think of anything or don't see anything in you! That's not the case - a lot of people want to give you a good answer and simply need time to do so. Remember: as awkward as you feel about "bragging" on yourself for this exercise, your friends may feel a bit awkward doing this, too, especially if you don't have the type of relationship where sharing "deep" things is commonplace. Additionally, we are all busy humans, so it's OK to follow up kindly after a few days.

Write down the responses and add them to your overall skills inventory as they come in.

Question Three - What Are (Or Can) You The Best In The World At Doing?

Some people can create a list a mile long when they're asked what they are - or can be - the best in the world at doing. Others will struggle because they are humble by nature and don't recognize their own value and contributions enough. Neither is wrong, although those with more skepticism tend to have an easier time eventually nailing down "the" thing in which they are the best.

What does "best in the world" mean here? While it could certainly mean the entire world - and I do believe there is something of value every single person has that no one else does - it stands for the world in which you operate.

Your "world" is the area in which you intend to do business. For example, if you plan to serve clients only in your local city, then that is your world. If you plan to focus on an industry, then that industry is what defines your world.

Take some time to think about this because it *will* have a very high payoff later on. If you're struggling because you don't think you're "the absolute best" or don't have proof, what could you become the best at within a *short period of time*? Odds are you can come up with at least a few items here.

For example, when I built my first specialty (what I call an "authority space" and which you'll learn about later) for airline pilots in my wealth management practice, I had proof I was good at providing financial advice to the general population. I also knew that if I invested 60 days in rounding out my knowledge with that demographic, I could be the *best* at providing financial advice to airline pilots. There's nothing wrong with being better or more versatile at what you already dominate in!

➢ What To Do If You Think Your Skills May Not Be Valuable To The Marketplace (Hint, It's Not True)

We *all* face a little self-doubt through a process as intense as building our own business from the ground up. That often happens when it comes time to take inventory of our skills, especially if we tend to be more on the reserved side or were raised to be "humble."

Even those who have no trouble coming up with a list of skills they possess can still let doubt creep in, wondering things like, "I'm good at this, but would anyone pay me for it?" and "Are there enough people out there that care about this skill?" If that happens to you, know you're not alone. But also know that it's OK to set that aside for now for two reasons.

First, because it's simply not true! You're likely being paid to do it already, and even if you're not, there are others that are, which means that a market for your skill(s) exists. Second, we'll walk through how to make it valuable to the right people later on.

For now, recognize that the skills you have are both valuable *and* enough for the marketplace. Also know that *you* are enough and *you do* have what it takes to get it done. You deserve it just as much as all of those who have done it before you, too.

➢ Summarizing Your Valuable Skills

There are over eight billion people on the planet, over 350 million in the United States, and probably a thousand times more people than you can reasonably serve within 50 miles of you.

The skills you have, including your primary skill, what you are (or can be) the best in your world at, and what others see in you all give you the freedom to create your own future. These skills are worthwhile and valuable to your market and to those you wish to serve, and there's a reason *you* possess that particular skill set!

By creating your skills inventory, you have a serious list of things you can do to bring value to the marketplace. In Chapter 5 we'll dive into defining (and locating) the right market for your skills, establishing your "authority space," and building *the* business for you to successfully do your own thing.

Hopefully you're starting to see the power of planning and laying out the details. The great part is we haven't even started getting into some of the most impactful aspects yet. Up next is taking an inventory of what's driving you to make this change so you have all the motivation you need to keep going.

CHAPTER

3

Your Motivations: Getting Clear On And Leveraging Your Personal Motivations For Breaking Free

Understanding the skills you have and how you can leverage them to break free and begin a life of successful self-employment forms the foundation of your journey. You build on that foundation with a clear understanding of *why* you want to make the change and *what* will keep you going when times get tough. That's what this chapter covers: your motivations for making the leap.

With any change we make, we are trying to "escape" from some level of discomfort so that we can "arrive" at a place of comfort[2]. In other words, we're always running *from* something and *to* something else.

---

2 I first learned of the "escape and arrival" framework from Frank Kern, one of my favorite marketers and someone worth checking out if you're not familiar with him.

In the opening, I shared my story and how I felt about staying where I was previously employed. For me, I knew that if I stayed the course I was on, I wouldn't be living up to my potential and my children would see that. It consumed me that I had a dream to be in control of my destiny, and that it was possible, but instead I was living for someone else's bottom line and selling my time to build their dream (instead of my family's). That's what drove me to create a plan and, ultimately, break free.

Knowing what's "below the surface," driving you away from employment and toward self-employment allows you to design a business that *serves* your life instead of *running* your life. Leaving just because you hate your job is the wrong long-term motivation, and you'll find that if you break out simply to "be your own boss," it will consume your life. You'll be your own employee *and* your own boss, keeping all of the headaches you have now while adding those of a business owner.

But, if you truly understand why you want to break free, and it's for the right reasons, then you can design a business that is ideal for the life you want to live. You'll draw on these deeper motivations to build and create your business throughout the rest of the book.

Please take the time to truly ponder your responses to these topics. No one is going to judge you for your answers and there are no wrong or "selfish" answers, either. In fact, your answers *should* be somewhat selfish, because this is for you (and your family).

I've found there are two types of motivations and drivers for why we want to escape employment and move to self-employed. First are the "short-term" drivers which don't go as deep and tend to be more focused on you (versus your family or lifetime impact). These are often dominated by what you don't like about your current situation and what your big dreams are.

Next are what I call your "long-term" motivations. These go deep down into more of who you are and what you want for your family and your overall impact on the world. Both are important, and I find that it's your short-term drivers that *get* you going while the long-term drivers *keep* you going when times get tough and struggles set in.

Your Short-Term Drivers

Your short-term drivers are what are readily apparent when you want to break free from employment. They focus on you and what you want (and don't) want more than they do on other people. That doesn't make them "bad" or lesser than your long-term drivers, because they are critical to the motivation to get going.

Short-Term Driver One - What You Don't Like ("Escape" Items)

This is the time to let it all out! Nothing is too "small" or "petty." Start with what you really dislike about being an employee. Get it all out and don't leave anything off your list. Doing so means you are being open and honest, not that you're "going negative" or complaining. These are your "escape" items, or what you want to leave (and will be leaving) behind. List them out now.

Short-Term Driver Two - What You Dream About ("Arrival" Items)

Once you have your "escape" items - the things that are pushing you away from being an employee, it's time to focus on what's driving you *toward* self-employment. These are your "arrival" items and focus on the positive things you hope for as you take control of your future and do your own thing. Nothing is too big here; this is your time to dream.

Whether it's time freedom, more money, making your kids proud, or being able to work with the people you want, get it all down. These items will be a key factor in how you build your business later on. List these items out now.

Once you have your "escape" and "arrival" drivers inventoried, it's time to understand your long-term true motivations. Remember, it's these short-term drivers that actually get you started on your journey and the long-term ones that keep you going.

Your Long-Term Drivers

The escape and arrival items you laid out above are important, but are also usually short-term in nature and can fluctuate with the environment and even your mood from time to time. It's your *long-term* motivations and drivers that tend to be the most powerful in your inventory. These might include family, relationships, core values, mission, hard-fought victories, and your legacy vision, among others.

If you have already built a family, this may be one of the most eye opening and powerful sets of exercises you'll do as part of this process. For some of the questions below, you may want to team up with those that matter most to you, such as your spouse and kids, and answer the questions as a team since all will be impacted and benefit from your move to self-employment.

If you don't have a spouse and/or kids, you still want to think long-term about the "whos" of your future, as well as those that mean the most to you now. Whatever business you ultimately build will not only impact the people in your life and future, but will also help you attract the right individuals to you.

Long-Term Driver One - Your "Whos"

Before you can leverage your long-term drivers, you need to know all of the "*whos*" that really mean the most to you. These are the people you want to enjoy life with and whose happiness is important to you. It doesn't necessarily mean the people that are *closest* to you, but those who mean the most. (Sometimes those aren't always the same).

You need to ask who *really* matters in your life? Who do you want to bring along with you on this journey? Whose life do you also want to make better as part of your move to self-employment?

The people that fall on this list - your "whos" - are called your "Family of Choice[3]," and are the individuals you care the most deeply about. They are the ones you want to build your life around, so it's important that your business aligns with and serves them, too.

Long-Term Driver Two - Your "Why"

Any discussion around "finding your why" is overused in business, almost to the point where it has been cheapened. That shouldn't be the case because your "why" is the reason you're here!

"Here" doesn't have to mean on this planet. It can mean why *you are where you are right now, thinking about breaking free.* What impact do you want to have? What do you really want to accomplish?

3 "Family of Choice" is a term I learned from Ryan Stewman's Apex Mastermind, something I believe is worth checking out. There are more details on the resource page at breakfreemoneybook.com/resources.

Who or what do you want to prove right/wrong? For whom are you contemplating making a change?

When we initially want to shift to self-employed, our "why" usually revolves around the negative (what we don't like about being an employee or our jobs). We think that it would all be easier if we were doing our own thing, if we were our own bosses, and those become our reasons for breaking free.

However, if you talk to any entrepreneur or business owner, he or she will tell you that things don't get easier at all. But, you get better at what you do *and*, if you have the right motivation, you're more fulfilled overall, which makes your *life* easier.

That motivation comes from understanding, deep down, why you want to do what you're doing. Why you want to make this change. Dig deep and understand *why* you really want to do this and make this move. I believe that comes from your mission, vision, core values, and the things you want to set in motion for others years down the road.

Long-Term Driver Three - Your Mission

A mission is defined as "a specific task with which a person or a group is charged" and "a definite task." It's something clear, specific, and easily understood and remembered.

Unfortunately, "mission statements" (like finding your "why") have been abused by corporations throughout the years. All too often we see big companies - perhaps even the one in which you are looking to escape! - misuse the concept as a marketing ploy or to try and build up a certain feeling in the employee or customer base. In almost all cases, these "only for show" or forced mission statements fall on deaf ears and prove ineffective.

Real mission statements, though, come from our hearts and describe the big, singular task we are working on and that we feel called to pursue at this point in our lives. They provide clarity and a framework for making decisions easily, even when times get tough. They even serve as motivators to keep us pressing forward when the world, life, and situations seem to turn against us.

In making the transition to self-employment, what are you really wanting to accomplish? What purpose do you want to achieve, and what is the overall aim or objective you want to reach over the next year, five years, and longer?

For some, defining the mission comes easily. For me, it was a struggle until I made it bigger than just me and turned it into a "family mission."

I hadn't thought much about a *family* mission prior to reading a great book, *Family Teams* by Jefferson Bethke. As I read through, I realized that our families (by blood/marriage or our Families of Choice) are the biggest parts of our lives and we are designed to succeed *together*.

Eventually, I concluded that since my business should *serve* my family and life, it made sense to start with a family mission. This is something I believe is true for you as well, if you're struggling with laying out what you really want to achieve as part of a personal/individual mission.

Talk with your family and determine what you most want to accomplish for them or with them. Once you have that, you can create your mission statement.

Mission statements don't have to be complex, so again, don't put too much pressure on yourself to make one for your family that seems "impressive." You want it to be *true, clear,* and *memorable.* At the same time, you want to make sure it's sufficiently narrow and direct to keep you on track as you build out your business. You're much more likely to have lasting success if it's designed in a way that fits your family purpose.

So how do you create a mission statement? By *having a clear picture of where you want to go and why.* Most of the time, it's about accomplishing part or all of something bigger than yourself, and rarely is it solely about money, although it can be for some.

For example, my current (family) mission is to *make sure we have time and economic freedom so we can do the things we want with and for the people we want, when we want.* Now, I have some deeply personal reasons and beliefs behind this, but it goes to show it's about the goals you want for your family, not something fancy to hang on the wall.

This mission paints a clear picture for me and serves as a "filter" for decision making within the context of my business that impacts me and my family. If an opportunity or time request pops up, I simply ask, "Will this help create economic or time freedom for my family?[4]" If the answer is yes, I will consider it. If the answer is no, I do my best to let it pass.

There will always be times when we get down, when the road ahead looks too far or too difficult and life seems to kick us around. In those times, we can turn to our mission statement and realize there's a bigger picture at play. That takes us out of our own heads and gets us back to work.

---

4 This ties in with my overall personal life mission of *helping people be financially and professionally free.*

As you create your mission statement, keep these thoughts in mind:

- It will likely change over time, several times, and that should be expected
- Work with your family (or Family of Choice) and make sure they are also comfortable and excited about it
- When you do, you'll find that you're all moving in the same direction
- Give it time! Keep refining it as you go through this process and you'll get there!

For ease, the below format can help you think through your family mission statement:

"We want to [what you want to do/help/guide/lead/teach/create/etc.] for [who you want to serve] so that [the benefit to everyone involved]."

This is the format I used for our family mission statement: *We want to create time and economic freedom for ourselves so we can do what we want, with and for the people we want, when we want.*

Start working on your mission statement now. If you're struggling, post in our Facebook group (facebook.com/breakfreemoneybook) to get some helpful feedback from others who are in your position. We're stronger together, and sometimes seeing what others are doing helps spark ideas.

Don't feel like you have to have this all the way nailed down before heading on to the next step, but remember, your mission impacts your family as much as it does you!

Long-Term Driver Four - Your Legacy Vision

For a lot of years, I would focus on the short-term and what I wanted for the next few months or, at the longest, the next few years. It took a lot of mentors, both in real life and through books, to get it in my head that such near-term thinking was limiting what I could accomplish.

I switched gears and started asking myself, "One hundred years from now, what do I want for my family? What do I want my grandkids, and their kids, thinking, feeling, and knowing about our family and what we pursued during our time here on earth?"

Here's a major lesson I've learned: *whatever you set in motion now will play out for 100 years or more.* Your life, your family, and your business have the potential to do some amazing things. If all goes according to your dream, what does 100 years from now look like to you? What will your family have become? What impact will your business leave? Will your name be known? Who do you want to have join you and what legacy do you want to leave?

Start writing down your answers to those questions and your overall vision. Once you have that vision, think about what it all means for you today. Because it's what you're building toward, having a clear picture of what you ultimately want will help you get started on the right foot.

It'll also give you the "long-term why" needed to push through the hard times and keep going no matter what. Because, at the end of the day, the only way to fail that vision is to stop pursuing it!

Long-Term Driver Five - Your Core Values[5]

What do you stand for? What are some of the "non-negotiables" you live by? Where do you draw the line, and what things won't you do for success?

Those questions help you get to the heart of what your core values are. Core values are the principles you live by and for which you stand.

One of the main reasons I see people wanting to break free from an employer is a lack of alignment in core values. Often, at one point, the company matched their values but no longer does (either through the individual evolving or the company changing). This creates internal conflict and often serves as a final "push" that leads to the change.

Gaining a better understanding of your core values not only brings clarity to why you want to leave, but also to what you want to build. Knowing your values will help you build a business that you love *and* that attracts the right people to you.

For example, my personal core values match with my family's and are: Freedom, Integrity, Resourcefulness, Responsiveness, and Meaningfulness.

We use these as "guiding lights" to measure our success and focus our efforts as we go through life. These are the things that are most important to us and keep us grounded. They have also served as the

---

[5] Tomas Keenan has a great book to help you nail down your Core Values called *Unf*ck Your Business*. I *believe* the origin of this all came from the great book *Traction* by Geno Wickman. While the concept of Core Values is largely meant for your business, it works great for individuals as well.

foundation for how I operate my business and how I "screen" for clients and people to partner with. (If you'd like to know more about these, check out breakfreemoneybook.com/familyvalues).

As you begin to think about your own core values, looking at a list can help get the ideas flowing. Simply do an internet search for "values" and you'll get plenty of helpful results to build your list.

Most people seem to quickly "click" with certain values and know, "that's me!" If you are one of those people, excellent! If you're having a bit of trouble, though, make sure you involve your family (or Family of Choice) in the exercise. When you nail down your values, you'll know it, and they tend to stay constant over time, too.

Once you feel like you have a solid list of values, add a sentence or two (no more!) to each so that you can quickly reference them. I even know some families (and a lot of businesses) that have them as artwork on their walls and I think that's an excellent idea to keep them front of mind.

For example, here are a few drafts of sentences to go with my family's core values:

- Freedom - to speak and live authentically; the only stress and weight we feel is self-induced
- Integrity - always do the right thing no matter what
- Resourcefulness - there is always a way
- Responsiveness - we are quick to act and respond
- Meaningfulness - do work that matters and "moves the needle" for others

Your core values are the non-negotiables and principles you live by and guide you as you pursue your mission, which will go hand-in-hand with your newfound business. They are also the bedrock of building a business that is true and authentic to *you* in every way.

Take some time, have some fun, and start putting together your core values. I believe this will be one of the most important things you can do for your business, financial, and overall quality of life.

Long-Term Driver Six - Reaching Your Potential

Sometimes our careers and jobs can get stagnant and we need new challenges in which to complete and "win." It's human nature to grow, stretch, and achieve, and often we're motivated to start a business so that we can reach a new level in our potential. While we should harness that and use it as fuel, we never want to forget that we are capable of winning!

Nearly every successfully self-employed person I know is motivated by challenges and reaching new levels. I think it's part of our human nature to pursue constant growth and realize our potential.

Spend some time thinking through who you want to *become* on this journey. What would be *the* ultimate victory? How do those tie into your other motivations and drivers above?

A person with a clear vision, articulated motivations, meaningful core values, and on mission is unstoppable. And all of this will carry over to the actual business you're designing, too, as you'll see.

➢ Summarizing Your Personal Drivers Inventory

Clarity is critical to building your business safely, wisely, and successfully. Going through these exercises, it's easy to wonder, "Why is all of this important if we just want to design a great business that's profitable quickly?"

The answer is simple: when you are crystal clear on what you don't like about where you're at, what's motivating you to push forward to something new, the values your family stands for, and the victories you've had so far, the right business is a lot easier to build.

If you pass over these exercises, your odds of building a business that is *not* congruent with you and your values is much higher and your chances of success are much lower. You're more likely to create a company that runs your life instead of serving it, leading you to resent it because it's not authentically "you." That's not a recipe for winning!

However, if you embrace these tasks, you'll have a better understanding of what you want, what you don't want, and what you're driving toward. Do the groundwork and start out strong.

Now, let's continue and build on this foundation of your perfect business!

CHAPTER

4

Designing Your Business To Serve You And Your Life

It's easy to get caught up in the excitement of starting a new venture and think that you'll "fix" any problems down the road when the time comes. From experience, I can say it's a lot better to design things properly from the beginning than it is to make corrections later on! That's what this chapter will help you do: design a business that serves your life instead of running your life. I promise you it will be time well spent.

When I started my first business with the goal of using it to break free from my W-2 job, I didn't take the time to build it *right*. I thought that the most important thing was getting money in the door *now*. In my head, if I got the dollars flowing in, I could figure the rest out later.

As you might imagine, I never did end up taking the time to "figure it out later!" I partnered with the wrong people for my goals, made costly decisions, and ultimately built something I couldn't stand and had to shut down. It was *worse* than being an employee.

Fortunately, I had a couple of good mentors who convinced me to take a step back instead of charging ahead full steam into something else I couldn't stand just to get away from my then-current job and "do my own thing." It's that advice, coupled with several other tools I've learned over the years, that has helped me build the right business for the right goals for myself and for others, over and over.

This chapter and the three that follow are about *designing* your business in a way that's aligned with your skill set, market, and "authority space," *and* that serves your life instead of running your life. All of those are important because they stack the odds of success in your favor over the short-term *and* the long-term.

Then, and only then, are you ready to actually *create* your business.

First though, there is nothing more important than designing your business correctly. I believe that if you put in the effort now to design your business the right way, *you will dramatically increase your chances of meeting all of your financial and personal fulfillment needs while building a business that serves you and your family instead of the other way around.*

Statistics tell us that the majority of new businesses fail within the first few years. The number one reason for that is a lack of capital (money available to operate). I'm convinced that the number two reason is that the business wasn't designed to be successful from the start.

There's no reason to build a business that the market doesn't want, that you're not qualified to run (based on your unique combination of experience, knowledge, skills, and background), and that you end up resenting. Those with a solid business plan always seem to do better than those without a plan when it comes to being successful, so let's make sure you are building this in a way that leads to success.

As you go through the next few chapters, you'll gain a clear understanding of:

- What you want your life to look like, once self-employed
- The right mix of your skills and experience for the market you're going to be in (called your "authority space")
- What to offer the marketplace to give you the best chance of immediate revenue *and* long-term success
- The ways you can test that offer before you launch so you have safety in the direction you're going

We will cover a lot of ground, but remember: *those with a plan do better than those without*, and that's what this is about.

➢ The Importance Of Making Sure Your Business Supports Your Life (Instead Of Running Your Life)

A couple of years ago I went to start a secondary business that was going to provide for our family after leaving my job at the time (the one I alluded to in the opening). While it took off financially (well into six figures a month of revenue) and performed better financially than I could have hoped, I absolutely hated it. I wasn't aligned with the right people for what I needed to build and didn't have the right processes in place. I still convinced myself that "as long as the money is there, everything will work out."

Instead of being my ticket to freedom, it made me miserable. Looking back, it seems so clear. All I focused on was, "How do I get income in the door, what do I need to provide to get it, and who can I align with to get me there quickly?" Even though I took the time to create and execute a plan that was financially successful, I failed to ask and account for the most important question: *"How can I make sure this business is something I enjoy and serves my life instead of running it?"*

Since then, I've made sure to thoroughly consider that question for every initiative I've started and everyone I've worked with, and it's made a world of difference. As tempting as it might be to throw everything into getting money flowing in, I believe you'll make that happen *and* create a business you'll love long-term if you focus on designing it correctly from the get-go.

To help make sure you stay on the correct path, use the following "checkpoints" to make sure your new venture aligns with what's most important to you. Then, once you've confirmed that it does, you will go about structuring your "Perfect Day."

Alignment With Your "Why"

In Chapter 3, you laid out your "why" as part of your long-term drivers. If you've figured out *why* you want to start your business, does what you're considering now align with it? If so, excellent! If not, you'll struggle to maintain the right motivation when times get tough, so consider how you can better fit what you're doing in with your "why." There's always a way.

Alignment With Your Mission

Looking back at your mission, ask yourself, "Is the business I'm building aligned with, and moving me toward, my overall mission?" It's easier to put in the required hours when you know your effort aligns with where your family wants to go. Not only is the support on the home front easier to come by, but you'll also be much more motivated to keep things integrated and pushing forward.

Alignment With Your Core Values

Making sure your business fits into and aligns with your core values is critical. If it doesn't, I would go so far as to say it's a "hard stop" and you need to reconsider what you're looking to do. There are few things that will sink a business faster than being out of alignment with your deeply seated values.

Take a few moments and revisit the core values you came up with previously and remind yourself of why those are so important. Then, ask yourself how you would feel if you weren't living by one or more of those values in your new business. What would the spillover effects be if you ignored a value?

For example, one of my core values is "Integrity." To me, it's about more than simply doing what's right and keeping my word, although that's a big part. What it really means to me is that if I operate my business with integrity at every turn, I can rest easy each night. If I were to compromise my integrity even slightly, I would have a tremendous unease about my business, how I was running it, and what the outcome would be. The guilt I'd feel would spillover to my family time and life in general. Because of that, I *never* want my business to put me in a situation to compromise integrity, so I've worked hard to design it around that perspective.

As you continue through this chapter, ask yourself, "How can I honor [Core Value] each day through my business?" for each one of your values. If you keep those answers in the front of your mind as you move forward, you'll come out with a business that syncs deeply with who you are and where you want to go.

Alignment With Your Legacy Vision

Next, ask yourself, "Does the business I'm building fit into my vision, and will it be a vehicle to *accelerate* reaching that vision?" If the answers are "yes," you all but ensure you're not setting yourself up to be in the same position a year or two or five from now. Focus on building a business you love and that supports your life and vision, and you'll be miles ahead - financially, in happiness, and in general - than if you bypass the process.

Once you've passed these "checkpoints," you're ready to think about what your best work day would look like. I call that your "Perfect Day."

➢ Your Perfect Day[6]

Your life is made up of a series of years, and those years are made up of months that consist of weeks and, ultimately, days. If you get each day right, you automatically get the weeks, months, and years right, and that sets you up to have the life you want.

In most cases as employees, the majority of our waking hours are made up of work. That sure doesn't change when we go out on our own, and often we're putting in even more hours in the early months and years. If you design your day properly, though, you can fit everything in and still maintain the energy you need to be successful at work and home.

---

6 I first heard this concept from a business coach of mine in the Apex Program, Drewbie Wilson. He introduced me to the concept and Craig Ballentyne has an excellent book, *The Perfect Day Formula*, about the topic.

If you *want* to work 12 hours a day, that's excellent and you should (so long as it doesn't cause issues with the other areas of your life that you value, such as faith, family, and fitness). If you only want to work four hours a day, that's also great. Whatever you want to do, though, should be done intentionally.

The best way to create an intentional life is to map out the details of your perfect day. In that map, you would lay out everything from when you wake up to when you go to sleep and everything in between. The point isn't to have your entire day dictated, but rather to make sure you set the limits and boundaries that you want while including what's most important to you.

There is *always* a way to make things work, so start with building your ideal day and then figure out how to put the pieces of your business and offer (which we'll cover shortly) together in a way that supports that.

How To Design Your Perfect Day

If you could design your perfect day, what would it look like? What time would you get up, what would you do first, and then what would come next? How would each hour look? Would you spend eight or 10 hours a day working, or only four? Who would you spend your time with throughout the day? Would each day be the same, or would you prefer different tasks/activities every day?

These questions bring clarity to how you want to run your day. One of my favorite truths is that "structure brings freedom." By having a clear structure in place each day, knowing what you want to do and don't want to do, it's going to be much easier to know *how* you want to serve clients and run the business you build. So take the time and write out your perfect day.

The first time I did this exercise myself, I had about ten things bulleted out. I shared it with a business coach I had at the time and instead of getting the praise I was looking for, he showed me his Perfect Day document. It was about four pages long and covered everything he did from saying "good morning" to his wife to what he did when he closed his eyes at night. That level of detail leaves nothing to chance, but it might not be for everyone, and that's OK. I ended with a happy medium between the two.

The most important part is clearly stating the boundaries you want incorporated in your perfect day. For example, if you get frustrated when clients text or call you in the evening during family time, then maybe you "end all client communication at 5 pm" and "set aside 30 minutes from 8 pm to 8:30 pm" to clean things up for the day. If you know you want to take your kid to school, put that in your perfect day too.

In addition to the boundaries, make sure you put in time for the things that motivate and "fuel" you. If you love to work out, then you need to have time allotted every day for it. The same goes with reading/learning; if that's important to you and it helps you be better, then it should have a place in your perfect day.

I've learned that being intentional and detailed (to the proper degree) has a powerful impact. First, it gives your mind a clear picture of what you want and it's easier to stick with as you go about building and operating your business. Second, it prevents you from finding ways to "cheat" those things that are most important to you. Third and finally, going into detail provides the "guardrails" for which to design your business. The clearer you are on what you want and don't want from each day, the clearer you are on the service(s) you'll offer and *how* you'll offer them.

To clarify: being incredibly detailed doesn't mean rigid and inflexible. My perfect day is one that isn't planned out to a "T" so that I have the freedom to choose what, when, and how I get things done. *But, I do make sure that there is time for what matters most and the right boundaries are set.* There are days I don't do great with it, and when that happens, I start fresh the next day[7]. It's a constant evolution, and the important point is to make sure you are running your day when you break free from employment instead of letting your day run you.

If this feels challenging, consider working up to it by adding a little each day, recognizing what you like, don't like, and what you wish was different. Over a week or so, you'll find you have a good template for what your perfect day can look like.

As you get your perfect day down, start thinking about how you'd implement it. What hours would you work, what would you do first, etc.? The most powerful question for doing this is, "What needs to be true for 'this' (my perfect day) to happen?"

You'll be surprised at how good it feels to know you can design a business that supports the kind of day you want. It takes work and it needs to be built (nobody will drop it in your lap), but that's what this process does for you.

Once you've confirmed that any business will pass the "checkpoint" test of your "why," mission, values, and vision, and you have your perfect day laid out, it's time to get to the tactical "hard" tools and processes to help you build the perfect business, and it starts with deciding what *you* can offer that no one else can.

---

7 Taking things a day at a time and forgiving myself and moving onto the next day was something I learned from one of my coaches, Nick Koumalatsos. He has a great mentorship program that I highly recommend.

➢ Summarizing Designing Your Business

Don't let the excitement and eagerness of starting a new business or chapter in your life let you get lax here! I've said it a few times already, but I'll repeat it here again because it's that important. *Start right and build a business that serves your life instead of running it.*

Overcome the temptation to "get it up and running" and then "figure out how to make it fit" later on. That rarely works out well in the end!

CHAPTER

5

Deciding What You Can Uniquely Offer to The Market

Now that you know what your Perfect Day looks like and have put some thought into designing a business that supports the life you want to lead, the next step is making sure you are crystal clear on what you can uniquely provide to the market. Getting this right gives you a big leg up to starting your new business with revenue on "day one" and ensuring you can be successful quickly.

Everyone I know that has gone through this process has identified something that they could uniquely do that was attractive to their market (the people they wish to serve). Each person was able to leverage their particular skill(s) in a way that set them up for success, and that's what this part is about.

This chapter is designed to help you boil down the options and identify the *best* service to offer and *who* to offer it to right out of the gate. When you find what you can uniquely offer to your specific market, you have found what I call your "authority space."

➢ Your "Authority Space"

If you've been an employee, you automatically know you have significant value to the marketplace. How else would an employer have justified paying you all that time? This should give you the confidence that you will be *at least* as valuable self-employed as you were as an employee. (Since you're one of the few with the courage to make the leap and build a plan, I'd venture to say you're *more* valuable out on your own!)

It took me years to acknowledge that I could be successful and provide something that enough people wanted and were willing to pay for. I knew to build the confidence and certainty I needed required me discovering what I was best at, what the market wanted, and building the exact right service for both.

I've since repeated that process several times and have seen many others do so, too. When you nail down what you can uniquely offer to the marketplace, you discover your "authority space" - the position you *own* in the world. Knowing this makes finding people that will pay you, and convincing them you can deliver, easier and more profitable.

It starts with a simple fact. *If you have ever created or done something valuable, there is someone out there who will pay to either learn how to do it or have you do it for them, too.*

(A quick note: if you've already decided what it is you want to do for self-employment, I'd encourage you to still go through the next three sections that cover the two main business models, how to discover what you can uniquely offer, and how to decide what business to ultimately choose. You may find a different angle you can take that will best tie into your market.)

The Two Main Types Of Self-Employed Business Models Built On Skills

While the possibilities are endless when it comes to creating a business that fits your desires, skills, and market, many people transitioning to self-employment fall into one of two broad categories: *consulting* or *coaching*. Both are similar and rely on your expertise. Understanding which you align most closely with will help you to narrow down the service(s) you want to provide.

In both coaching and consulting the "product" you are offering is your expertise (the combination of your experience, skills, background, and knowledge). What differs is *how* you deliver that to your clients.

Coaches often provide expertise and general action steps to their clients but do not help on the implementation of those suggestions. In other words, a coach may provide information and guidance to an individual, though he or she does not help that person take the action. Consultants, on the other hand, usually either work *with* the client as he or she takes action and completes the task or actually *does* the task for the client.

Both are valid business structures and both can deliver worthy results to clients. I know very successful people in both camps, and there are people who "blur the lines."

How do you decide which one is for you? You will usually find people focused on scale and reducing time spent with clients gravitate toward the coaching sphere as it is usually less time intensive. For those that prefer to work one-on-one with clients and are focused on making sure the individuals (or businesses) get the desired results by implementing the recommendations, consulting tends to be the most common path.

One isn't "right" or "better" than the other. It's about how you feel you can create the most value for your clients and how you want to spend your time and structure your business. One final difference I've observed over the years: coaches often cover at least a slightly broader range of topics whereas consultants tend to stay fairly specific and "narrow" on their offering.

For most people breaking free and starting their self-employment journey, the consulting path is usually the easiest to get up and running, especially if you don't have a big list of people who follow you currently. The reason is you can often operate closely to what you've been doing as an employee, which means you are already familiar with the work that can and needs to be done for clients.

As time goes on, you may find a desire to scale, and that's where switching to a coaching model can come in handy. You may find that you can help more clients by sharing your expertise and recommendations (but not executing alongside/for the clients), or you may discover that you can help other consultants improve their work.

There are plenty of possibilities, but to help you make the transition, the remaining sections will focus on helping you identify your ideal consulting niche. Why? Because that's the "fastest path to cash.[8]"

Now it's time to find out what business you are uniquely suited to begin your path as a consultant.

---

8 It was a coach of mine, Drewbie Wilson, that helped me understand the importance of finding the "fastest path to cash."

➢ Discovering What Business You Are Uniquely Suited To Build

There is an intersection of the value you can provide and a demand in the marketplace. In other words, there's something you are capable of doing that fills a need in the market, which means someone will pay you for it. Once you discover what that is, you have likely found a business that is suited just for you, which dramatically increases the odds of rapid success.

To identify what that niche might be, you want to leverage your primary skill that you decided on earlier and think deeper about *how* you can provide that skill to your market. The best way to start narrowing these down is to gain clarity on the following items:

- The specific problems you can solve for people or businesses
- The questions around your skill(s) or expertise that you are continually asked
- Where the intersection of your (1) passion, (2) talent, (3) spirit/gut, and (4) market need is
- What you want to become "known for" in this world

As you go through those items, make sure you're keeping in mind your Perfect Day and how each option may or may not support the life you want. Take your time through this section because it's the key to finding what you will create and offer the marketplace. (We'll cover identifying that perfect market following this).

Identify The Specific Problems You Can Solve For People And/Or Businesses

Start by listing out the problems you can help people, businesses, or families solve. People pay for solutions that remove discomfort and problems, so when you're the one that does it, you are in a position to collect income in exchange for solving those issues.

Start by clearly understanding the problems your primary skill solves. If you're a CPA, for example, you might solve the problem of making mistakes on tax returns or paying too much in taxes. If you're a general business consultant, you may identify gaps your client doesn't see and provide ways to close those, saving them money and time.

If you plan to do something similar to your current job or role, think through your last several tasks or clients and think about what problems you solved for them. List as many as you can and see if there are any additional "gaps" or challenges these people have that you might be able to fill or solve.

The real power is that as you build your list of problems you can provide a solution to, you also begin to see *who* you can serve. Then, it's simply a matter of finding where those people are and sharing what you do. More on that shortly.

Identify The Questions You Continually Get Asked Involving Your Skill(s) And Expertise

Consider what people tend to ask you regularly. Almost always that serves as a clue to where you can provide value and make an impact.

Have you ever felt like people always ask your advice about a certain topic (or topics)? That's because those people see you as an expert and a trusted source in that area. If there's a topic or series of topics that continue(s) to come up, you've likely found your "authority space." *That* is the area where you can be *the* person in the market.

Pay close attention and observe what people ask you and what others say about you over the coming days and weeks. These people can be peers, clients, or potential clients, it doesn't matter. The key is capturing those comments and understanding how it might be your authority space. You'll be surprised how often you've brushed it off as either not important (in your eyes) or just part of a normal day[9].

Identify The Intersection Of Your Passion, Talent, Spirit/Gut, And Market Need

This exercise can help you think objectively about what you really love to do, what you're good at, what feels "right," and what the market needs. If you can find the intersection of those areas, there's a *very* good chance you've found what you could uniquely offer.

Your Passion - What do you love doing?

What parts of your current role do you like the most? Are there things you do in your job that feel effortless because they are so easy and enjoyable? Do you find certain tasks that are fulfilling because of the impact you have? If so, you're likely honing in on your work passion. Make a list of things you truly enjoy doing.

Your Talent - What are you good at? (Your primary skill and what you're the best in the world at)

While being passionate about what you're doing is powerful, you should also be good at it! That's why you want to find passions that

---

9 It's often the case that the things we're really good at or have expertise in seem so common to us that we brush it off as "normal." This is a version of "imposter syndrome," where we don't think our skill set or expertise has value. Nothing could be further from the truth, and that's likely why people turn to you!

overlap with your talent. "Talent" is equivalent to your primary skill and what you can be the best in the world at. When you combine something that falls into your skill set, that you're good at, and that you love, there's a good chance you're onto your business idea. Write down the talents you have as part of your primary skill and make note of those that overlap with your passions.

Your Spirit/Gut - What is your conscience telling you to do?

When you have that "little voice" in the back of your head prompting you to do something or move in a direction, often there's a reason. Whether you want to call it your spirit or your gut or something else, there's a good chance it's guiding you in the right direction. The reverse is true, too: if your gut is telling you something is wrong (which is different than being nervous or fearful), you may not be considering the right business. Think about the possible combinations of your passions and talents and write down any that "jump out" at you and seem to strike a nerve.

The Need - What does the world need that matches your passion, talent, and spirit/gut?

You can love doing something, be great at it, and feel it's the right thing to do, but if there's no market or need for it, it will be difficult to achieve financial success. That's why we focus so heavily on combining all of these elements. While we'll identify your market shortly, remember that if you're currently getting paid to do what you plan to do when you transition to self-employment, there's likely a market need now. Review your passions + talents + gut/spirit, see where they might overlap, and identify if the combination links up to a potential need in the market.

Identify What You Want To Become Known For In This World

If you are passionately pursuing self-employment, it's likely you have a desire to do something bigger than yourself and want to "make your mark" in the world. When you have those thoughts, and considering what you've done so far, write down anything that comes to mind about what legacy you'd like to leave.

For me, I felt a pull to change a few things in the wealth management industry that I thought were outdated and unfair to clients. That became a driving force as I finally left employment to start my strategic wealth planning firm. It wasn't about pride, but about the *impact* it would have if I was the person that helped make those changes.

You may not have an answer to this one now, and that's OK. If you do, though, it may be a clue as to your unique authority space.

➢ The Power Of Offering Only One Service

There's a good chance the last several exercises (and your own thoughts throughout this process) have you narrowing down what you can uniquely provide to the marketplace. You likely have several options to choose from as you do, and it can be challenging to pick just one.

I believe the temptation to start with multiple services to offer clients comes from wanting to "expand your footprint." I can say with confidence that you'll be better off choosing a single offering when you launch. Doing so allows you to focus your efforts and concentrate on making it successful. Committing to a lone option can be intimidating, but remember that you are able to pivot at any time, and as long as you're operating within your skill set, you'll be able to adjust quickly if needed.

To do that effectively, you're going to want to understand what one skill would give you the best chance of success and break it down even further.

How To Narrow Your List Down To One Service

When you choose a service that aligns with your primary skill and expertise, you stack the odds in your favor and set yourself apart. To get there, break down your potential options into their smallest components. Here's how to do it.

The first step is to reduce your top skill down into the smallest element you can. For example, if your primary skill is "sales," identify the specific area of selling where you shine. You might be the best at software sales, and then, even further, business-to-business software sales. Perhaps you even specialize in startup business-to-business software sales.

That process of breaking down your primary skill to a very "niche" level allows you to capitalize on one area in which you can focus all of your energy. (Startup business-to-business software sales in our example above). The more narrow your skill that you'll build your business on, the easier it will be to market and create your offer (the next two topics on deck).

After you've narrowed down your primary skill to the smallest possible niche, determine what area within that subset you're most passionate about. For our startup business-to-business software sales example, it might be "finding new prospective clients." If that's something you love doing and are good at, you've found a good overlap that can launch you out of the gate. (Every company wants more prospects and, as a consultant, you can show them how to get those clients, you'll have a clear "path to cash").

Once you've narrowed down your skill and verified it meets all the criteria above, it's time to identify the best market to enter. You do that by breaking down the market into the smallest possible elements just as you did for your skill previously.

➢ How To Select The Right Market

Your market is the group of people (or businesses) that might benefit from what you do and are likely in need of your services. It's made up of the people who are actively looking for someone like you and what you bring to the table (even if they don't know it yet).

While finding that market might sound like a tall order, there's a systematic process to identify the individuals or businesses who would benefit the most from your service. Take this part seriously because, short of running out of money, the two biggest things that could derail your success are not taking action (which we'll talk about in Chapter 12) and *going after the wrong market.*

The first place to start is the market you're serving now, especially if you plan to perform a similar task or remain in the same field as you are currently serving. If you're planning to do something different, the exercises that follow will bring clarity and confirmation as to the right market to go after.

Either way, and even if you plan on operating in a different field or service, you'll likely still be using a skill set (your primary skill) that you've honed and practiced before. That means you will have at least *some* familiarity with the people you'll be serving based on that experience.

Your Current Market

You may already know quite a bit about your current market if you plan to stay in the same field in which you've been employed. If that's the case, it's time to get even more familiar with the people you'll serve since you have more at stake running your own business.

Regardless of the track you find yourself on, you'll be better off the more you "niche" down as far as you can go within your market (much like we did with your skill set previously). Doing so will allow you to start quicker (which means more revenue sooner) and make it a *lot* easier to design the perfect offer and service for the people you plan to serve, which makes them more likely to want to work with you!

Niching down is also important because of a very real fact: Your current employer is larger than you will be on "day one," which means it can offer broader services to more people than you reasonably can. *But*, that is to your advantage! A large company might do more in general, but you will do *more for your perfect market* than it could ever hope to do. The best way to win this game is to find one small sliver of the market that you can dominate in and pursue it passionately knowing you are *the* best option for those clients.

For example, my last job as an employee was at a national wealth management firm. While the company served anyone and everyone needing help, I made an effort to narrow down into a few niches. When I left to go out on my own, I further refined it to people with very specific considerations.

Not only did this give me more credibility in the space because it was "all I do," but it also made it easier to identify the right people to market it to because they had to have the specific considerations we were solving for, along with the other complementary wealth management needs. My previous employer couldn't do that simply due to size, so it became an advantage to me.

Regardless of which market subset you decide on, invest time to thoroughly understand it and what the people in it need. Identify what is working well for them now, what could be better, what keeps them up at night, and what they would be starving for that you could provide. If you have good relationships with some of those people now, ask them what's missing and what they would benefit from the most. Document their responses and leverage it as you build your offer in Chapter 6.

There are tons of different ways to build knowledge of your market and as long as you end with a good understanding of *(1) who they are, (2) where they are located, (3) what gaps they have, and (4) how you'll connect with them*, you'll be ready to serve people well.

Feel free to use the "Who Is My Market?" sheet in the resources center (breakfreemoneybook.com/resources) and fill out each section. Anything you don't have the answer to right now, research, ask around, and do whatever you need to do in order to obtain the answer. Knowing more about the subset of the market that you want to serve will give you every advantage as you plan to build your business in the next chapter.

Let's dive into each of those four criteria.

Who Can You Go After?

The first thing you need to answer is exactly *who* the people in your market are. In other words, *who,* specifically, should you go after? The people you want to approach need to be both accessible to you (otherwise you won't be able to make them an offer or serve them) and have some sort of costly challenge or "gap" in their life (or business) that you can uniquely fill. The key is to identify that small "niche" or subgroup of your potential market where you say, "I know *exactly* where to find them."

More often than not, you already know the broad "whos" that should form the base of your new clients because you: (1) are currently working with them, (2) were them/were where they are in the past, or (3) have intimate knowledge of either their business or life.

If there are certain groups or subgroups of your market where you have no connection, background, or knowledge, it's going to be much harder to reach them and find similar ground. On the other hand, if you share similarities and are comfortable with the group, your future conversations are going to be much smoother and, ultimately, more profitable for all.

As you prepare to launch your business, keep in mind you may not be finding your "perfect" clients right out of the gate. You might have dreams to work with a certain clientele, and you should always pursue that over the long-term. In the early days, however, keep it practical and focused on who you can easily identify and those to which you have ready access, knowing you will eventually be able to pursue and serve the people you want.

Where Are They Located?

Knowing the right people to approach is critical, but it only goes so far if you don't know where to find and connect with them. The days of cold calling (and even cold emailing) are gone, so you need to find a group that you can readily identify where they spend time and gather.

Do the people you want to serve hang out in Facebook groups, or are they at local country clubs? Are they part of a business or trade organization that you could join and have a narrow group to reference? Do they share a common activity or education? Who do you know that can get you involved with your ideal "whos" as you launch?

When I was designing one of the earlier versions of my wealth management practice, I knew I wanted to work with airline pilots because I had a certain expertise and ability to do well by them (and they are generally a blast to work with). I quickly realized there were several subsets (based on age, airlines, seniority, etc.) and I needed to narrow my focus.

I found that if I stuck with two particular airlines, I could locate my market through a couple of existing connections, their unions, and a few different podcasts and publications they listened to and read. I did that and was a guest host on one podcast, appeared on others, and wrote for several publications, which all led to more prospects than I could serve - a very good thing! We'll talk more about leveraging those strategies in Chapter 7, but the important point now is that I had to understand *who* the right group was and *where* they were "hanging out" (and *how* I would get to them).

I believe the best decision you can make as you launch into self-employment is to decide to serve a group that you can locate and approach. If you're not sure how to gain access, find a trade group, mastermind, or other program where your target clients pay to be included. I held back on doing this for years, and when I finally made the switch, I quickly realized not only was it a faster and easier path to those individuals, but they also were willing to pay to improve their situation.

What Gap(s)/Challenge(s) Do They Have?

Everyone has challenges and "gaps" in their life and business that they want solved and filled. When someone comes along with a solution that removes the challenge or closes the gap, those people are often willing to engage with and pay the individual for that solution. That's the essence of what moves the economy *and* businesses forward.

When I built a second version of my wealth management practice, I had a particular belief that "good values and good investment returns were *not* mutually exclusive." In other words, you could invest in companies whose business models and practices aligned with your particular values and still generate great returns over time.

I realized there were plenty of people who wanted to invest their money in alignment with their values, but most people had slightly different prioritizations of what was "right" from a conscience standpoint. Doing a little homework, I learned that the challenge these people all collectively experienced was that they had to invest for the future but their current investment portfolio held companies with values or products they didn't agree with and they knew it.

I also found that there was a big gap in the market: *no one was offering custom mixes of stocks and bonds designed to a client's particular values.* There were plenty offering one-size-fits-all strategies, but nothing directed exactly to the client's wishes.

It was that challenge (seeing their investment dollars fight against their values) and gap (no solution to knowing with confidence and transparency their investments could align with their conscience) that allowed me to add sizable recurring revenue in a short period of time. All I had to do was find the gap and challenge it created and bring a solution that addressed it. I did that by offering a custom mix of investments that were put together just for each client's unique financial needs and values.

So, as you look toward your market, take the time to break out what challenge(s) and gap(s) the people in it are experiencing and verify that your primary skill set can fill those gaps. If you struggle to find challenges or gaps, go back to the "whos" and dive into another subset of your market and try it for them. Doing so will pay off in multiples as you launch.

How Will You Connect With Them?

The "catch" is that everything you've done so far will only work if you're able to connect with your target people. As long as you plan out how you will approach your market first, though, you should be able to capitalize on all of that effort.

There are two main paths to connect with the people you are aiming to serve: direct and passive. Directly connecting with people occurs when you know the person you're aiming to meet with or can be introduced by someone else who knows you both. (Think of a referral arrangement or a target client or customer you know).

Passively connecting comes when you do something and those people reach out to you. (Think of being a podcast guest and it leading to people contacting you afterward or running ads to reach a broader audience and collect more names). Both have a place and we will get into specifics in Chapter 7.

The important point now is that you are certain there are at least three or four good paths you can take to reach your target clients (even if you don't have the specific trail to get there yet). Personally, I've always leaned on what I feel is the easiest (and fastest way to generate income): working with someone who already has your ideal people as an audience or clients. I call these "referral partners" and we'll cover how to set those relationships up in Chapter 7.

Make sure you've answered the classic "who, what, where, and how" questions to make sure you're pointing in the right direction as you launch your new business, setting you up for success from the get go.

➢ Summarizing What You Can Uniquely Provide And Your Market

Take your time in this section and go back through it all again if you aren't sure you're on the right track yet. The more confident you feel on both the service you will provide and also who you will provide it to, the better you'll be as you move forward!

When you're ready, it's time to tackle your offer.

CHAPTER

6

Creating And Testing What You Will Offer The Market

At this point, you know *what* you can do for your clients and *who* your market should be. You're ready with the service you plan to provide and have broken it, and your target clients, into as small of components as you can. That means it's time for you to create your offer, which is how you articulate that information to your ideal future clients in a way that gets them to say they're interested in hearing more.

You create the right offer by testing it and, if needed, adjusting and refining it. This allows you to gain insight from your ideal market about whether they would accept your offer or not, and what, if any, things you should change about it *before* you go full-swing into your business. That's what this chapter will do for you.

A word of caution first if you're already feeling "ready to go." It's critical you have everything in place to deliver on the promise you're making in your offer. You don't want to do all the work to create a compelling offer and fall flat when it comes time to deliver it. Nothing can hurt your reputation faster! Now, let's get your offer up and running.

➢ Creating Your Offer

The first step in creating your offer is to decide what it is you're bringing to the market. This is the service you came up with in the last chapter. For example, if you're a CPA and you have decided to target entrepreneurs focused on personal development, you will need a different offer than a CPA focused on hospital employees, simply because your target future clients have unique needs that require different communication.

Crafting your offer is about articulating what you do clearly so that potential clients or customers understand what's in it for them. It's about being able to sit down with someone and giving a solid explanation about what you do and how you can help them. At the core, it's about *them,* not you or even what you do. It's about the *outcome* to them and how they will benefit.

When you start crafting your offer, keep in mind *you don't need to make it "salesy" or slick sounding now.* You'll work on spicing it up as you go. At this time, it's about getting the main concept nailed down. Here is a simple "task" to help you think about what you will do for your market, which will then help you in the offer process.

These are the things I will provide for my market (list as many as you can think of):

____

Once you have a list that you feel comfortable with, you want to consolidate everything into one statement that lays out the main benefits you provide. This sounds tricky, but once you play around with it a bit, you'll see it start to come together. We'll continue on with our CPA example below.

In our example of a CPA targeting entrepreneurs, you might decide that you'll help clients save on taxes, get their books in order, create profit and loss reports to track their business, calculate estimated payments, and so on. When you boil it all down, you find that what you really do is help your market "reduce their tax headaches and bills while staying out of the crosshairs of the IRS."

Working on this offer statement will be one of the best time investments you make. You'll get more comfortable as you go. Refining your statement is part of the process and will only help you be more confident in your "pitch."

Once you have your "one sentence" statement, you need to turn it into a formal offer. While there are many different techniques, the one I've found to be the simplest (which is often the most effective) is the "How to ____ Without ____" format.[10] It looks like this:

How to [get something your target client wants] without [doing something he or she doesn't want to do].

It really can be that simple! Here are a few examples, starting with our running CPA example:

"How to minimize your business and personal taxes and associated headaches without landing in the IRS's crosshairs."

"How to escape your employer and become successful doing your own thing without risking your family or savings."

"How to legally and ethically save 100s of thousands in taxes over your lifetime without landing on the IRS's radar."

"How to get your investment holdings to match your values without compromising returns or the environment."

Each of the previous examples can be written any number of ways. As you go through this exercise, write out several versions of your offer statements and you'll start to find a few that "click." You're likely to come up with several before you land on one that's "it." Once you do find one that you feel is strong, simple, and likely to be effective, you want to test it out with your market.

[10] While many have taught similar approaches, this became clear to me working with Ryan Stewman in his Apex Entrepreneurs Mastermind. I've included a bit of information about it in the resource guide.

➢ Test And Refine Your Offer

Testing your offer simply means you put it out there to a small sample of your ideal market. This allows you to get quick feedback and make any adjustments before you launch.

The best way I've found to do it is with a simple "If I, would you?" question posted to social media or shared via email or text with people who are close to your ideal clients.[11] It looks something like this:

"[Ideal person] - If I created a [guide/course/service/etc.] that [showed/did/helped you/etc.] [big benefit/what they want above] without [thing they want to avoid or hate], would you want to take a look?"

That's it! Here's a quick example:

"Tax preparers and CPAs - If I created a simple three-page guide that showed you how to deepen your client relationships and reduce the workload you had during tax time without having to expand your services, would you want a copy?"

"Business owners! If I created a program that minimized your tax bill without landing on the IRS's radar, would you want to take a look?"

"Exhausted employees, if I put together a 30-day program that gives you everything you need to break free from your employer and launch your own business without risking your savings or putting your family in a bind, would you want to be a part of it?"

It sounds simple because it is! You're not trying to sell them anything here because your business isn't built yet. It doesn't have to be fancy

---

11 This concept was also brought to my attention through Ryan Stewman's Apex program.

or slick because at this point you're only gauging the interest of the market. You want to get your offer in front of at least a dozen or more people in your ideal market to test it.

How do you find those people? If you already have some type of email list, you can leverage it. If you don't, consider tapping into social media. If you can't post on your personal page (due to wanting to keep your plans under wraps), find a couple of Facebook or LinkedIn groups that match your target audience (they are out there). Take a few days and add some value by commenting on posts, providing sincere compliments, and sharing some insights. Then you can either ask people through direct messages or, once you clear it with a group admin, post your test question.

Keep in mind that any list of people you build to test your offer with, online or offline, becomes a group of potential clients for you down the road, so treat them respectfully and thank them for their time. You may even find a few that are *very* interested, so take time to start building those relationships!

Based on the feedback you get, you'll either discover you nailed it on the first go (which is rare but possible!) or you need to do some refining. Ask follow-up questions to those who say "no" (or even nothing at all) to identify what they might like to hear instead. For those that say "yes," thank them and ask what it is they like about it and if there is anything else they'd like to see.

Take that insight, adjust your offer, and then test again. You'll be amazed at how quickly this refines what you're building and how your perfect clients can actually help you design the right service to offer.

➢ Structure Your Offer To Bring In Revenue "Day One"

The best offers not only attract your ideal future clients, but also position you to bring in revenue immediately upon launch. I call these "day one" offers because of their design to generate income right out of the gate.

You need two things to create an effective "day one" offer. First, you need a list of interested potential buyers so you know immediate demand is available. Second, you need your service fully established and ready to fulfill so that you can complete your sales and delivery cycle in short order.

The best way I've found to build a list of interested potential buyers ahead of launch is through (1) the people on which you tested your offer, (2) people you know from your past, and (3) any leads and "authority followers" you've created (more on that in Chapter 7).

To make sure you have your service set up and you're ready to deliver on your offer, start building out your process now. Make sure you have all the resources in place and know exactly how you will provide it to the client. This allows you to focus your time and energy on acquiring clients and simply executing your service instead of having to "figure it out as you go."

The unspoken benefit to having both of these things (a list of potentially interested buyers and your process built out) is that you'll have a *lot* more confidence when you do launch. Because you know where your first buyers are coming from and exactly what you will do for them, much of the pressure is off and you'll be able to keep your focus on doing what you do best.

➢ Keep Your Offer Simple!

When we start creating an offer, it's natural to want to "expand" what we say we can do to try and attract more clients or make our offer sound grander than it realistically is. If you find yourself in that position, reverse course quickly and make sure that you really can deliver on the actual product or service behind your offer.

You need a much smaller subset of the market than your gut will tell you at first. "Casting a wide net" sounds good on paper, but it makes it *much* more difficult to target the right people and be certain of the service you will offer. Likewise, you are good at what you do and there's no need to try and market yourself for something beyond your core skill set or service.

I always say "the truth is good enough." This means that whatever you're skilled at and whatever your true offer is really is good enough! There's no benefit in over-embellishing or trying to force yourself into more than you are easily capable of doing *from the start.* Nothing will destroy your confidence or reputation faster than overpromising your capabilities or what the client will get. As long as you stay well within your wheelhouse, the rest of these techniques should put you exactly where you want to be: successfully launching your self-employed business.

➢ How To Stay On Track And Create Long-Term Clients And Fans

I believe the key to staying on track and creating long-term "fans" is to make sure you have your entire process buttoned up *before* you launch.

Over the years I've seen a surprising number of people wait to build out their service until they start serving their first client. To me, this is both inefficient and unproductive because it forces you to take time away from growth and potentially deliver a less than stellar experience.

I know there are many "gurus" teaching the "figure it out as you go" philosophy, but it's a recipe for failure (and certainly one for greater stress)[12]. You're much better off testing your offer first and then, once you've found the correct one, having your service fully built out and ready to go by the time you launch.

This is especially important because failing to have everything mapped out in advance will put a lot of pressure on you *and* it risks your effectiveness and reputation on the first client or customer. If you hurt that reputation because you weren't ready or you didn't have your procedures lined up, it'll set you back *and* rock your confidence.

You're going to have to build your system and procedures no matter what, so do it *before* you agree to deliver something to a client. I learned this the hard way, twice, so please let me save you the cost, heartache, and embarrassment and suggest you be proactive.

Bottom line: if you build your business structure properly, correctly identify your primary skill, choose the correct market, and design the ideal offer for them, the only way you can fail is to mess up delivering the service. Get that right, and you're set!

---

12 There are a lot of "coaches" out there who will tell you to "sell it first" and "build it as you go" and that way you make sure you don't "waste time or money" on something that the market doesn't want. That works sometimes, but it sure isn't the safest or most effective way to do it. I've personally seen that those with systems always do better than those without, *especially* when you're delivering it in the current form for the first time.

➢ Summarizing Designing The Right Offer

When you know what you're offering and to whom you are delivering it, set about creating your formal offer to the marketplace. Lay out exactly the services you'll provide and how you will do so and then translate it to a simple "How to...Without..." framework. Test and refine your offer, building your list of interested people along the way.

Adding those pieces together and ensuring that your service and process is fully operational at launch should position you to succeed *quickly* when you launch. There's no better feeling than having a check rolling in "day one!"

Once you know what you're going to offer and how you plan to provide it, it's time to build your authority and get some clients!

CHAPTER

7

Establishing Authority And Getting Clients

A business without clients won't last very long! That part is obvious, but what can be less obvious when starting out is that there are plenty of ways to get clients in the short-term (and even more strategies over the medium- and long-term).

I've seen newly self-employed people make the mistake of not balancing short- and long-term client-getting strategies. Too much focus on getting clients "now" and you won't have a steady flow of future clients months (and years) down the road. Solely focusing on long-term client-getting strategies such as building authority and content could leave you pressed for cash for the first several months.

This chapter addresses how to get clients early on and how to build authority with your market for the long-term so you always have a steady stream of clients open to doing business with you.

➢ The Basics Of Finding Clients

A full scope of sales and marketing is well beyond this book, but a few definitions will help you get the most out of the information that follows.

First, a *lead* is a name with contact information that you can reach out to in order to see if he or she is interested in what you offer. A *prospect* is a lead that has "raised his or her hand" and shown interest. A *client* is someone who has signed on and decided to pay you for your services. Your *"authority space"* is the niche you can own where you are *the* person in your market.

Starting out your client-getting efforts by creating resources and expert content for your authority space will get you going on the right path *and* make your life easier in the months ahead.

➢ Your Authority Space And Creating Resources

The first time when I started putting together the "final touches" on my first truly successful business, I was nervous about getting clients. Would people come? Is what I have good enough? All of those questions played out in my head. When I sat back and thought it through, though, one thing gave me the confidence - and ultimately the results - I needed: Realizing that I really was *the* person in my space with what I was offering clients. Not in a conceited way, but as proof that I had dialed in (and down) my offer and service to such a degree that it was accurate.

I believe the same will be true for you, too. When you are operating in your authority space, you immediately gain confidence and recognize that you really *can* make all of this work.

I've had the opportunity to start four different practices in the wealth management space and two ventures in the publishing and book writing space. One thing I learned the hard way is that *you must find your own tiny spot in the market and absolutely dominate it.*

For the people I worked with that have written an "authority book" (see breakfreemoneybook.com/authoritybook for more information) and gone on to build a business based off of their expertise, knowing their "spot" has been the biggest driver of their success.

By now you know exactly what you want to offer and to whom you will offer it. Let me ask you a question: Do you *own* that space? Are you *the* person for that particular service (or product)? In other words, are you the authority for what you're bringing to your market?

If so, then you have found your "authority space." As the name implies, it's the spot in your market where you are the absolute authority. No one else comes close. Now, if you're not sure or that sounds like too much of a leap, know that you can "plant your flag" and *become* the authority. Nobody is born as *the* person in a space; someone claims it, owns it, and delivers for the people inside of it.

Being the authority simply means you are *the* expert, the person to whom everyone should turn on a particular topic. So as you prepare for your launch, ask yourself the most important question you possibly can:

What needs to be true for me to be the *authority in my space?*

Write down every answer you come up with, prioritize them based on (1) how big of an impact it will have on your launch and business and (2) how quickly and easily you can get it done. *There will be no more important task than this as you launch your business.* Everything else needs to be done of course, but this is the *one lever* that can drive massive success in the short-term for you.

The biggest lesson I've learned throughout the different initiatives I've taken (both as an employee and self-employed) is that *you can be the authority in a space right now; you just have to "niche" down or refine your offering far enough.* As you seek out a smaller audience within your market, you start to find who you can be *the* person for today. Once you identify that space, start claiming it by creating content and offering help.

I really believe the best way to claim your space is through content, and in particular, writing. The root word of "authority" is "author" and this means as soon as you begin authoring content on something, you become an authority on it. When you've authored more valuable content than anyone else, you become *the* authority. That's it. Below you'll learn how to turn this into the biggest lead generator you will have, so really give it some thought.

You don't have to be a "writer" to produce this content. You simply have to share what you know about the space and solutions for people who have some of the gaps or challenges you identified in the last chapter. If writing isn't your thing, you can do videos, podcasts, speaking, etc., too.

If you are struggling with the type of content to produce, one thing that will help is getting crystal clear on the transformation you'll provide. To truly be *the* person in your space, you need to have a defined benefit and impact to those you wish to serve in your authority space.

➢ The Transformation You Provide

A transformation is something that moves an individual or business from one position to another and leaves him/her/it in a better place. It doesn't mean you have to change someone's entire life completely, but it does mean that you've moved him or her - or the business - forward in some way.

Don't make the mistake of failing to recognize and appreciate the impact you're having on the people you are serving! Just because what you do seems simple or normal to you doesn't mean it is to others.[13] I promise you there is tremendous value there, so take a step back and objectively look at the impact of the transformation you're providing.

Being able to visualize that transformation is important because you need to be able to make your clients see it, too. That's what communicating it is all about.

Communicating That Transformation

There are many high-quality resources out there on improving your communication, selling, and articulating a vision. To keep things simple, I've included a formula below that you can use when you're sharing your transformation to your potential future clients. The clearer you have it in your own mind, the easier it'll be to share with those you would like to serve.

Remember: Your goal is to move your clients from "Point A" to "Point B," leaving them in a better position than before they met you. It really is as simple as that. The best way I've found to articulate that is with the below formula:

---

13 Remember the "imposter syndrome" concept we talked about before? Where something comes so easily to you or you're so well versed in it that you begin to believe no one would value your expertise? Just remember, that's the "imposter syndrome" playing tricks on you, and it isn't true!

We help you [eliminate a headache or do something useful] so that you can [do/have/experience/etc.] [the thing they really want].

You may notice that it's similar to the offer statement you made earlier. That's because you want to align it with your successfully tested offer, and because it ensures you stay in your core area of focus.

This formula keeps things simple and helps you better communicate your value. It'll get you started, but never stop learning or striving to improve how you articulate it *and* deliver it.

Here are a couple of examples for you:

We help you select and manage investments that align with your values so that you can grow your wealth knowing you're doing the right thing with your money.

We give you the tools to become the most elite version of yourself so you can live a better and more joyful life.

We help you reduce taxes so you can keep more of what you earn and retire earlier.

It doesn't have to be "smooth" or "slick," but it does have to be clear. Practice writing out your transformation and how you might articulate it to your potential customers and clients.

➢ Generating Leads And Building Authority

Up to this point you've been getting ready for launch by designing your business and understanding the various service processes you will provide. One big question remains, and that's "Where will my clients and income come from?" There are many options to land clients, and they all share a single thing in common: *their success is dependent on the level of action you take.* That's good news, though, because it means you have control of your success!

In the resource guide (breakfreemoneybook.com/resources), I've laid out some of the best programs I've found that help you think about generating leads, marketing, and selling and closing. The intention here isn't to recreate those, but to share and simplify what's worked well for me to consistently get clients both at launch and over the long-term.

Leads And Where To Get Them

A "lead" is an individual that has provided you with contact information and "opted in" to your world in some way, shape, or form. He or she may have found you through your authority content, referrals, marketing, advertising, or any number of options. Your lead might or might not have an interest in your service at this time, but did provide a method for connecting or staying in touch (such as email or phone number).

It took me *years* to learn that there isn't a shortage of leads in the marketplace. I used to think they were scarce, but I quickly learned that once I was clear on what I was offering and who would benefit the most from it, many opportunities opened up and my access to potential clients was limited only by my creativity and willingness to put in the effort.

Remember, there are over eight billion people on the planet, and more than 330 million in the U.S. In fact, there are likely more than you can handle in your industry or location. There's no shortage of leads, only a shortage of clarity on who you can help the most and what you will provide. *That* is why you've focused so heavily on those items before this point.

Below are some of the strategies that I and others have had success with over the years. I've always been the kind of person who *hated* the feeling of imposing on people, so you'll see that the kind of leads I tend to generate are of the "opt in" variety, meaning they saw something of mine they liked and "opted in" to having me contact them. (Of course, cold calling and similar strategies can work for some, they're just not for me and most cautious-type entrepreneurs).

Leads Through Authority Assets

"Authority assets" are items of content that you create (or have someone create for you) that demonstrate to your market and ideal clients that *you* are the expert and *the* authority in that space. Some examples include:

- Your own blog (and social media feeds)
- Articles you have published online or in print (think of the "as seen in" tags you see)
- Videos you've made
- Courses you've created
- eBooks and print books
- Podcasts you've been on or published
- ...and anything where you "showcase" your expertise[14]

What should you talk about when creating your authority assets? The things on the minds of those in your market! What are the people you're targeting wondering about and what do they need to know? Where does your field of expertise (your primary skill) overlap with their needs?

---

14 Coach Micheal Burt's Monster Producer program was where I first heard the term "showcase event," which is any event or situation where you are able to get in front of many people at once. (This is also covered in his *Legacy Selling* book).

I like to use the "objections" or "considerations" that my market has to generate content ideas. These not only speak to what might be on their minds, but also allow me to start to overcome sticking points that they may have with doing business with me (or my industry).

For example, if you're a CPA targeting new entrepreneurs starting to scale their businesses, your market may have the following considerations:

- Am I going to have to pay other taxes if I hire someone? What do I have to pay? And when/how do I do it?
- What forms do I need to file with the IRS?
- Can I deduct everything having to do with an employee?
- Will I make my money back with an employee?

Which means you could create content that addresses these questions. Mix in several topics that you know are important and that might get their attention, too. Here are a few more examples:

- How to solve the four biggest tax headaches when you start hiring employees
- What all can you deduct when you hire a new employee?
- When you should, and shouldn't, provide benefits to your employees (and how to best deduct them)
- How to pay for your next employee with tax savings

These are just quick examples, but they should give you an idea of the format using your market's objections and considerations. The process is to first find out what your market is concerned about and the objections they would have for your service. Then add in the things for which they are searching answers and use those items to create your authority content and assets.

This approach will keep your "pipeline" of content full while making sure you stay focused on *them* and not what *you* do (which puts you miles ahead of the competition who only talk about themselves).

The most powerful authority asset I've found and used is a printed book. People don't typically throw books away, and they are the ultimate sign of authority ("author-ity" - get it?). They convey expertise and give you a chance to highlight many different ways you can help and provide value.

When I wanted to create an offer to serve airline pilots in my wealth management practice, I put together a book and self-published it on Amazon. I wasn't a natural writer (though I had the knowledge for the content), and it took work to get done, but it opened a lot of doors for me and established me as *the* guy for the space (as it was the only book about the specific topic at the time).

I went out and found the leading podcasters and publications in the space and almost always was able to schedule meetings with them (and eventually was brought on to talk and contribute regularly) once I mailed out my book to them. They quickly saw that I wrote "*the* book" on the topic and it made life a lot easier for me to get in front of the right people and potential clients.

I learned many lessons through that process (both what worked and what didn't), and since then, I've been alongside dozens of authors who went on to do the same. Each of those individuals has had the same success with their books as "door openers" and, ultimately, a way to generate more than enough leads. It's amazing what an opening of "I literally wrote the book on that" can do for you. Like anything though, it requires the investment of time and energy up front, but it *is* worth it.

Even with the effort required, you can do it efficiently by compiling your book while you create your other authority assets. As you write articles, blog posts, longer social media posts, and record podcasts (and transcribe them) in preparation for breaking free, you're building a library of content that can be linked together and form your book.

Whatever you create doesn't have to be perfect. It simply has to show that you are the expert, allowing the person holding your book or reading your article to say, "Wow, this person gets me and what I'm going through." You'll be surprised how long those assets can stay relevant to the market and generate leads for you because they last forever. Once you create them, they pay dividends for years to come (and in the case of books, often additional royalties).

My favorite thing about printed books is the number of "doors" they can open. The "door" that has yielded the most success over the years has been with excellent referral partners.

Leads Through Referral Partners

Finding ideal referral partners is the number one way I've found to establish income quickly while launching a business. Done properly, your clients are much better off for receiving a more holistic solution and the individual or business who referred the client to you wins, too.

Referral partners are people who already have access to your ideal clients and market, and would be willing to introduce you for a percentage of the revenue you make. I like to think of these individuals and businesses as a "contract salesforce" because they help drive revenue to you and you compensate them for it.

To be clear, these are not "kickback arrangements." Referral agreements are formal and disclosed to the client and your role is often filling a gap in the referrer's business. The person introducing the client to you functions as a salesperson for your company, and that is clear to the client. "Kickbacks," on the other hand, are under-the-table payments that go unnoticed, unreported, and undisclosed to clients. Referral setups are the opposite because they are transparent and ensure that everyone wins, especially the clients.

After I published my previously mentioned book for airline pilots in 2016, I started to have people ask me how I did it. Each time I would share what I did, but in 2018 I had a mentor that wanted my direct help through the process of getting his book out to the world[15]. It was an enjoyable and enlightening experience and we took the model we used together and turned it into a publishing company.

While we had a solid model and delivered a great product, I didn't know very many individuals wanting to write a check for $15,000+ (the going price for the service at the time) to become an author "now." I did know a *few* people who wanted to be an author, so I helped them create a great book for well less than the $15,000 price point, which allowed me to create a "proof of concept" and additional confidence.

In particular, I went to a business coach whose program I was participating in with a few best-selling book examples in hand and worked out a deal to help his coaching members write books and become best selling authors. I quickly received more clients than my small publishing team could handle at the time (which forced us to learn to scale), and he received one third of the revenue. Most importantly, the clients/coaching members became best selling authors with best selling books, which, as you may now know, is one the best lead generation and "door opening" tools around. Everyone won.

---

15 That book is *God Wants YOU to Win!* by Shane Rudman. It went on to become a #1 best seller in multiple categories and has a powerful message.

More recently, I've been able to leverage referral partners in my wealth management practices and know dozens of others that have launched a company with revenue from "day one" simply by establishing quality referral arrangements. The key is to be willing to share and, as one of the coaches in the Apex program says, "make sure everyone eats." When you do that, everyone wins, especially the client. The best part is you have a thoughtful way to earn income immediately without having to drum up a significant amount of business.

Invest some time now and identify who has access to your perfect clients already. Come up with a good reason why you can help them and create a fair agreement. Then, *show* those people exactly what you'll do for the clients they refer to you, how you will uphold their reputation, and what they have to gain. (By the way, one of the best ways you can show these people that you will do everything the correct way is by offering a glimpse at your well-constructed Standard Operating Procedures, or SOPs. More on these later).

Here's an example of going *far* to prove how you can benefit a referral partner. Before even bringing up the idea of creating books for my business coach's clients, I took one of his online courses and turned it into a physical book. Without anything else, he immediately saw that I could deliver, and once learning we'd do it under his brand umbrella, he was all in. Then, we went about proving the concept and helping a lot of incredible authors get their messages out and businesses growing. Effort pays off.

If you have your authority content and a couple of good referral partners in place, your likelihood of securing income right as you launch your business is high. Focus on delivering a good service, keeping your word, and over-caring for your clients and you'll be set in the longer game. The core of which is, for me, funnels.

Leads Through Funnels (The Long-Term)

"Funnel" is one of those overused words these days, largely due to internet marketing. In the broadest (and most old-fashioned) sense, a funnel is the path that someone who has never met you or heard of you takes until he or she either becomes a client or is removed from your list.

The top of the funnel is where people first meet you and, in this case, "opt in" to give you permission to follow up with them in some way. The bottom of the funnel, or the end, usually means where that person decides to become a client or not.

There are hundreds of programs and books out there that teach marketing, and you'll find the list that has impacted me the most on the resource site (breakfreemoneybook.com/resources). What we are talking about here is simply building one or more paths that people can take to find out about you and, if it's a potential fit, request more information on becoming your client.

I've had the best luck with very simple funnels that offer something of value to individuals (I've used books, self-made calculators, and special reports) in exchange for their name, email, and sometimes their phone number. These valuable items are called "lead magnets" because, when done right, they will attract leads like a magnet. And I can tell you that you don't need to be especially skilled at marketing to make these effective - I'm living proof!

(I only "bought into" these simple funnels once I saw them working well for dozens of members in a few of my mastermind programs. I never liked the feel of the "upsell" funnels I'd seen on the internet, so I was skeptical that they would be too "salesy." That's when the "give value and keep it simple" strategy was introduced to me. Since then, I incorporate that into everything I use.)

All you need to have a successful "give value and keep it simple" funnel for clients, in my experience, are the following:

- An attractive domain name that ties into a part or all of your offering
- A simple two-page "funnel" website where:
    - The first page offers them your lead magnet (the valuable item) in exchange for name, email, and perhaps phone number, and
    - The second page is a "Thank You" page where you thank them for accessing/downloading your lead magnet and let them know what to expect (or do) next[16]
- A follow up system to provide value and see if they are a fit (discussed shortly)

As you build your authority content, you'll create resources that can serve as a lead magnet for your funnel. Combine that with getting it in front of the right people and you'll start building up a nice email (or phone) list that you can stay in front of and continue to offer useful information. Eventually, you'll find that people are at a point where they need what you can provide them, and since you've already provided value, they'll reach out. That's why these often work best as a "long-game" strategy, because they can take a couple months or more to become effective.

When I first started incorporating funnels, I noticed two things. One, you could adjust it almost endlessly and, two, no one was just showing up! I quickly learned that funnels aren't "build it and they will come" tools. That can actually be to your benefit in the long run, though, because most of your competition will give up at this

[16] Another shoutout to Ryan Stewman's Apex mastermind here for helping me realize these don't have to be complex and that simple is usually better.

point, leaving you with an advantage. If you stick with it and find ways to get people to your funnel link, you'll build your list and set the stage for a full "pipeline" of future clients. (More on building your list in a moment).

As far as the potential for endless refining goes, make adjustments when you're sure it'll be of benefit and then observe the results. But, I've come to believe that as long as you provide a high-quality lead magnet and good content to the right people, you'll be OK. Just give out something valuable, tell the truth, and the rest should take care of itself.

The more challenging aspect quickly becomes *how do you get people into your funnel?* Once you learn a couple of techniques, it really becomes an easy long-term play.

If you're working on your authority content through articles, blogs, videos, and even a book, simply make sure your funnel link is in each. If you're on podcasts or other "stages," reveal your funnel domain name (website address) when asked "Where can people find you?" This technique has been the most effective for me and I still use it nearly every day. In my experience, it's the single best way to build a large "list" of people interested in your content that you can follow up with which, ultimately, leads to business.

For driving people to funnels online, I was behind the curve for a long time. In the last couple of years, though, I've learned and implemented the most through Ryan Stewman's Apex program and its "Build Your Machine" process (link in the resource section of the website). In short, you can leverage social media (Facebook, LinkedIn, etc. - wherever your ideal clients are) to post your authority content and connect with people there.

I've found that engaging in groups, whether on Facebook, LinkedIn, or offline, is a great way to add value to others. When you're constantly engaging with helpful (not salesy) comments and providing value in these groups, people want to know more - and they feel like they already know you!

Online, they'll check out your profile and that's a great place to have your funnel. You can also offer up any guides, reports, books, etc. you have to people through direct messaging on the platforms (again, don't do anything salesy or spammy!). Offline, find the local groups where those people tend to gather and, frankly, just be a good person. Don't worry about driving business, just be nice and provide value where you can and you'll be surprised how well it works. (I speak from personal experience on this!)

Finally, make sure your funnel link is in your email signature, on your business cards, and anywhere else you can place it without it being obnoxious to your target clients.

Once the people get in your funnel, you'll want to focus on following-up with them on a regular basis to show them you are someone of value that can solve their problems. That's where a good follow-up system comes into play.

➢ Follow-Up System

Your follow-up system doesn't have to be complex. You simply want to have a systematic way to keep "in front" of the people who give you their contact information and show interest in what you're offering. While it's likely the vast majority of your initial business will come from referral partners and directly targeting people with your authority content, your follow-up process is a longer-term strategy. That's all by design as it allows you to diversify your revenue sources over time and, eventually, have a steady flow of qualified clients.

The reality is that, at any given time, the majority of people who might be interested in what you're doing aren't ready to come on as clients immediately. A good portion of them potentially will one day, though, and that's why it's important for you to be there at the top of the inbox (and mind) when the time comes.

Because of that, the "core" of your follow-up system is usually an email list, as that's what most funnels will capture. There are plenty of resources out there around what to do with an email list, but the short version is that I believe you need to be sending regular (at least weekly) helpful and relevant content that benefits and speaks to your ideal clients. That's the key to staying in front of them.

In addition to an email list, I like to have a "CRM" (customer relationship management) system to manage the information provided through the funnel. These systems allow you to keep a record of potential future clients' information and set tasks to call, follow up, or meet with them. I learned the hard way to take really good and detailed notes of the conversation, too, so please do that. (It's amazing how that helps months down the road!)

The best follow-up system is the one you use, so see what others are doing in your industry and model what is working for them. Then add your own style to it and stick with it. Where your authority content and referral partner strategies can get business going immediately, your follow-up process will carry you long-term.

➤ Turning Leads Into Clients

Once you have leads coming in and begin to establish those relationships, you want to make sure the correct ones become paying clients. I've included the best "sales" programs I've personally had a chance to review and implement in the resources guide (breakfreemoneybook.

com/resources), so this part is a high-level overview of what I've learned about converting potential clients to actual clients as a newer self-employed individual in a startup.

The biggest thing to remember as you go into sales meetings with potential clients is that *you are bringing value.* Sure, the client will be the one writing the check, but you've built up the years of experience, thought through every aspect of your business, and are clear on the transformation you will provide. You're the expert and the one putting money in his or her pocket. Both of you are valuable, and you both can benefit from doing business together.

I don't mean that to sound ego-driven at all. I just know through experience that it's easy to get caught up in our own heads when first trying to take on new clients as self-employed. We'll talk more about making sure your mind is "right" in Chapter 12, but for now just remember, you are the expert!

The best way I've found to prove to people that I can help is to actually *show* them I can help them by adding value to their lives. Too many people - including your competition - think that the work starts once someone becomes a paying client. I understand the argument that it doesn't make sense to put in all of the effort before you get paid, but often doing the opposite is more profitable in the end.

Instead of telling someone all of the things you can do for them, find a way to show them. For example, in my main wealth management practice, we build out a full financial plan with every strategy we'd recommend laid out clearly for clients, including tax, investment, legal, risk, income generation, etc. (coordinating with their accountants and attorneys when appropriate) and share it with them before even asking them to become a client.

What this does is powerful. First, it shows them that we care and we listen. Second, they see right in front of them in real time the impact we can have in serving them, both in dollars and extra time. Third, it differentiates us from the competition. Fourth, it builds trust because they see "behind the curtain" on how things are done. Fifth, and finally, it shows them that to implement through us is turn-key (and it'd take a lot to start over).

Because we do all of the work upfront, potential clients are impressed and actually *see* that we're the experts and can help them. Sure, we could have just told them all of that information and explained what we offer, but which do you think builds more certainly in their minds? Of course - showing them.

How do you build out a "show don't tell" strategy for what you do? First, if the service you provide allows for it, actually do some (or all) of the work for them before asking for a thing. If that's not possible because what you do simply can't be done in advance, then build an example for someone just like them and show how it works. Over time, you'll end up with a bank of examples that you can use for other clients based on their similarities, so the extra upfront work becomes less over time.

The benefit to the client is that they immediately see you as an expert who can help them. This makes it easier for them to make a decision. This has the added bonus of making your job a lot simpler if you're not a salesperson at heart! You don't have to convince them of anything because your work does it for you.

(Keep in mind that, even if selling isn't your "thing," you can generate new business better than the best "closers" simply by having the real deal behind your offer. That's why it's so important to design your business and SOPs in a way that you know provides the transformation you're selling to clients. Potential clients will see that and have confidence you can deliver.)

My best recommendation is to always be growing in your sales learning and training. Whether or not it comes naturally to you, *everything* starts from sales. The better you are, the more business you will do *and* the more impact you will have because you'll be better at "selling" them on taking the right advice for their lives. Put in the effort here and you'll be thankful as time goes on!

➢ Summarizing Building Authority And Gaining Clients

You can design the best business and service in the world, but if you don't have clients, you aren't going to make it very far. Hopefully, you've seen that it's easier to attract new clients than many expect. Start building up your authority content, create your lead generation systems, and then master one selling strategy (such as showing potential clients what you do, like I do) and get to work.

Everything is coming together with your primary skills, ideal business design, offer, and process for getting new clients. You're getting close to breaking free, but before you do, it's time to position yourself financially for your launch. Your move to self-employment should put you in a better financial position, so let's make sure that happens now!

PART 2

Getting Your Financial House In Order And Establishing Your "Financial Runway"

CHAPTER

8

Your Financial Inventory: Getting Clear On What You Have And Where You Stand Today

You've focused on building out your business so far and now it's time to start talking about your money. More specifically, how to make sure you are in the right financial position as you break free and launch your business.

This is about *how to* make sure you have things set up correctly, not *whether or not you can* or should break free. That's an important distinction because there is *always* a way to make things happen. You don't need to have a million dollars in the bank to safely break free, but you do need an awareness of where you stand and an iron-clad plan.

Once you know where you *really* stand, you have a starting point that you can build from and, ultimately, reach your "break free freedom point" in a way that keeps both your financial future and family as secure as possible as you take the calculated risk to launch.

(A quick note before we begin. You will see several references to "level one" and "level two" as we go through your assets, liabilities, income, and expenses. Remember this as you go through: *level one is what you should focus on.* That is the "real" level that's relevant to your financial runway and future. Level two numbers are ones you should calculate as a backup and for full awareness. That will all make sense shortly).

➢ What Makes Up Your Financial Position

There are two main components of your personal financial position: your net worth and your cash flow.

Your net worth refers to everything you own minus everything you owe. Essentially, it's what's left after you add up all of your assets and subtract all of your debts/liabilities (net worth = assets - liabilities). It's the number that drives everything in your financial life - from the flexibility and security you have now to the way you are able to live in the future.

Likewise, your cash flow is simply a record of all of the money you have coming in (your income) and the money you have going out (your expenses). When you subtract your expenses from your income, what's leftover is called your "free cash flow" (free cash flow = income - expenses). It's the "extra" that you can save, invest, and use however you'd like.

As you take financial inventory of your life for the purposes of safely and smartly moving into self-employment, you are going to focus mainly on your *assets* and *expenses.* Your liabilities and income certainly matter to your financial well-being and over the longer term, but for the sake of creating your break free plan, we will focus on assets and expenses.

When you add up your net worth (assets - liabilities) and cash flow (income - expenses) below, you will separate things into two levels to better clarify the process. Each level will be explained more in the following sections, but know that "level one" will be the key to building your financial runway and "level two" will give you a reference for a worst-case scenario.

(As a reminder from earlier, your "financial runway" is a measure of how long you can pay your bills and live your life without income coming in. The goal is to make sure you have income right out of the gate with your business, but prudent planning ensures you know your runway).

In a few short steps, you're going to have a clear picture of what your financial situation looks like, and from there you will be better positioned to maintain your financial stability as you break free.

➢ Finding Your Net Worth

Recall that your net worth is made up of two components: your assets (everything you own) and your liabilities (everything you owe). Assets increase your net worth and liabilities decrease it. We'll start by breaking down your assets and then move on to do the same with your liabilities.

Asset Breakdown

If you're a "by hand" person, grab a pen and paper. If you prefer a simple spreadsheet that you can keep and update, head over to the resource area (breakfreemoneybook.com/resources) and pick up the free Google Sheets version. (*Quick note: I'd recommend going with the Sheets version as it has a lot of what we'll be doing together and will handle much of the math for you*).

Step One

The first thing you're going to do is list out all of your assets. Don't worry too much about order or what type they are yet. The important thing is to write down the big things you own. (No need to document the smaller items for this exercise - it's the financial accounts, vehicles, home, investments, collectibles, etc. that matter).

Step Two

Break out the assets into "level one" assets and "level two" assets. Level one assets include financial accounts that you can readily access with little or no penalty or tax impact. These can include:

- Cash in the bank
- Investments outside of IRAs or 401(k)s that have not gone up significantly beyond what you paid for them (which minimizes the "tax cost" if you were to sell)
- Life insurance cash value
- 401(k) assets (as there is a tax-free way to access some of these funds for your business)
- Roth IRA assets (specifically, the total contributions)

As a reminder, these assets - the level one assets - will be your primary focus.

Level two assets include those assets that can be available within a couple of weeks but might incur a penalty, major tax impact, negative cost, or significant reduction in value if sold in a hurry. These are your backup assets and might include:

- Investments outside of IRAs or 401(k)s with large taxable gains
- Retirement plans or IRAs that could be cashed out (it's not recommended to actually do this, but we are tracking it to have awareness only)
- Life insurance cash value that could be surrendered
- Home equity
- "Extra" vehicles or collectibles

Don't worry too much about what we'll do with these at this point; we are just getting them recorded so we have them all in one place.

Asset Name	Asset Value	Asset Level
Cash in the bank	$25,000	1
401(k)s	$350,000	2
Investment accounts	$125,000	1
House	$450,000	2
Cars	$28,000	2
Collectibles	$10,000	2
Other savings account	$5,000	1
Roth IRAs	$36,000	1

Liabilities Breakdown

Assets are one aspect of your net worth equation and liabilities (or debts) are the other. In addition to breaking them down into "level one" and "level two" liabilities like you did for your assets, you'll also identify which ones carry the most burden. This gives you insight on where to focus your efforts to improve your financial runway. (Enhancing that runway is discussed in the next chapter).

Step One

Start by listing out all of your liabilities. These are your debts - the things and money you owe. Also include your monthly payment next to each (so you have the total amount owed plus the amount you have to pay monthly).

Step Two

With each of your liabilities and their respective payments listed, calculate your "Payment Pain" ratios. Doing so is a quick process that tells you which debts have the biggest bang-for-the-buck in getting rid of first. We are doing this because a liability with a small total balance but a big payment is one we want to get rid of first so it can better position you financially for your move to self-employment (a deeper explanation to come on this shortly).

To calculate your Payment Pain ratio for each liability, simply divide your monthly payment by the total balance of that debt. That number is a percentage and it tells you how much of the balance you are paying each month. (Side note: this does ignore interest, but for the sake of your near-term financial runway, that's OK!)

This step is best done using the Google Sheets spreadsheet on the resource website (breakfreemoneybook.com/resources) as it's already automated for you. That being said, and if you prefer to do it by hand, here's an example.

Debt: vehicle payment
Balance: $15,000
Monthly payment: $750
Payment Pain ratio: 5% ($750 / $15,000 = 0.05; 0.05 x 100 = 5%)

The debts for which the Payment Pain ratio is the highest are the ones you'll want to consider eliminating first as you build your financial runway. We'll get to building and enhancing that runway in the next chapter, but before we do that, we need to categorize your liabilities. (As a reminder, this process is what gives you the power to break free sooner and safer!)

Step Three

Now it's time to categorize your liabilities the same way as we did with your assets. *Keep in mind that "level one" and "level two" are just for your reference here. Level one liabilities are the ones that will have the biggest bang-for-the-buck in getting rid of as you break free and build your financial runway.*

Level one liabilities are those that have a high overall Payment Pain ratio, such as 8% or higher. These are the ones that really take a hit out of your monthly cash flow *and* could potentially be paid down earlier based on the lower overall balances.

Level two liabilities are the ones that have a low overall Payment Pain ratio, say 5% or less. (The ratios between 5% and 8% can fall either direction. I tend to place them in level one ranked by the ratio). These debts are ones that, on a relative basis, don't carry as much "pain" as the ones with higher payments relative to the balance.

These "low pain" debts are the best ones to keep while you're in the process of breaking free because the cost to maintain them is much lower (and easier to handle each month) than ones with a higher Payment Pain ratio. Keep making your payments, of course, but you'll want to focus any extra paydown on level one liabilities.

Liability Name	Balance	Monthly Payment	Payment Pain Ratio	Liability Level
Car loan	$10,000	$50	0.50%	1
Credit cards	$4,500	$725	16.11%	2
Student loan	$26,000	$850	3.27%	1
Mortgage	$350,000	$4,250	1.21%	1
Personal loan	$50,000	$5,000	10.00%	2

Paying off your level one debts (the ones with the highest Payment Pain ratios) can increase your "financial runway," which is how long you can last without income when you break free.

Where do you draw the line between "high" and "low" Payment Pain ratios? You have two options here: (1) simply split it down the middle, which works well if you have several outstanding liabilities, or (2) choose a percentage number as a cutoff.

To keep it simple, any debt you have with a Payment Pain ratio over 5% can be considered a "level one" liability. Anything under 5% would usually be considered a "level two" liability because it is a lower burden on you.

What about the different interest rates? Good question. They do matter, especially over the long-term. All else being equal, we want to tackle paying down high-interest rate debts first. This is the most efficient and profitable way to eliminate debt, when debt elimination is our goal.

In the context of breaking free and launching your business, though, paying down debt is not the immediate goal. The immediate goal is to put your *cash flow* and *assets* in the best position possible to give you plenty of financial runway to be successful.

You'll also find that the higher the interest rate a given debt has, the greater the Payment Pain ratio. This occurs because having a higher interest charge on your debt increases your monthly payment, which increases the Payment Pain ratio.

If you can eliminate one or more of your high Payment Pain ratio debts, that not only frees up cash flow each month (meaning your financial runway is extended), it also can be a very good long-term use of assets.

Primary Net Worth Trackers			
	Total Net Worth	$588,500.00	

Total Net Worth Breakdown			
Assets		Liabilities	
Level 1 Assets	$191,000.00	Level 1 Liabilities	$386,000.00
Level 2 Assets	$838,000.00	Level 2 Liabilities	$54,500.00
Total Assets	**$1,029,000.00**	**Total Liabilities**	**$440,500.00**
	Total Net Worth	$588,500.00	

Summing Up Your Net Worth

Nice job of calculating all of your net worth details! The next chapter will show you how to make the most of this information to extend your "financial runway" as you head toward self-employment so you have a stronger foundation for your launch.

Before we calculate your cash flow figures though, there's one major benefit to being self-employed that you simply don't get as an employee: a potential boost to your net worth. When you build a business you are *creating an asset!* Your business will likely have value in and of itself, which can make it a contributor to your net worth. Not a bad deal!

➢ Getting Clear On Your Cash Flow

Your cash flow consists of two components: income and expenses. Income is any money you have coming in from wages, investments, tips, royalties, etc. Expenses are the dollars you have going out to cover housing, living, etc.

If you have more income coming in than going out, your cash flow is "positive." If the reverse is true, and you're spending more than you have being paid to you, your cash flow is "negative."

Mission number one is to always be cash flow positive! That's true both in your personal life and in your business and is the single biggest determinant of how much you can do and are worth over the long-term.

As you prepare to launch out on your own, a positive cash flow can be used to lengthen your financial runway. This happens when you allocate your "extra" cash flow toward savings or authority assets. If your cash flow is negative, now is the time to change that using the strategies to be discussed in Chapter 9.

Let's break down your cash flow.

Income Breakdown

Step one is listing out all of your income. Then, we'll break that into two categories: income that will remain when you leave your current job (level one) and your total current income *now* (level two). Bear with me here on these levels - they will make more sense as we dive into your "financial runway." Additionally, it's your *expenses* that will have the biggest impact as you break free, but income is still important.

Step One

First, using whichever method you prefer, list out all of your income. This would be anything you have coming in, even if it may go away when you break free. Some sources to consider:

- Your current employment income
- Spouse's/partner's income (if applicable)
- Investment income such as dividends, interest, etc.
- Side-hustle income
- Rental or lease income
- Royalties such as books, software, etc.
- Gifts (if they regularly occur)
- Anything else that is somewhat regular in its occurrence

Step Two

Once you have a list of all of your income, it's time to break it down into level one and level two, just as you did with your assets and liabilities previously. In this case, level one refers to the income that will remain when you launch your business. Level two is *all* of your current income.

Add up all of your current income from a monthly standpoint. If you have certain dollars that come in once a year or every few months, divide those out so that it's a monthly number.

For example, if you get a gift of $1,000 each November, then divide $1,000 by 12 to get $83.33 a month. If you get $600 every quarter (which is every three months), divide $600 by three (since it's every three months) to get $200 a month.

To find your level one income (the income that will remain after leaving your job), copy your working list and simply remove what will go away when you move to self-employment. Odds are, this includes the biggest source - and potentially almost all - of your income. If that's the case, don't worry! That *is* the game plan: Replacing your employment income with self-employment income that *you* control.

It can be intimidating to see the income "disappear," but remember that you will build that income back up as your business grows. At this point, the goal is to get a real picture of the income that will remain once you leave employment. (And it may even be refreshing knowing that something will remain).

Once all of your income is laid out, it's time to break down your expenses.

Income Name	Annual Income Value	Income Monthly Value	Income Level
Salary	$375,000.00	$31,250.00	2
Side hussle	$20,000.00	$1,666.67	1
Investments	$1,000.00	$83.33	1
Gifts from people	$3,000.00	$250.00	1

Expenses Breakdown

Getting clear on your expenses can feel overwhelming, but it gets easier as you get going. You most likely have many transactions that occur in any given month and the idea of tracking each of those can sound like a burden at first.

The good news is you don't need to track *everything* for the sake of building your financial runway. You do, however, need to be aware of how much you spend and where it's generally going. Fortunately, there are several options to do this quickly.

You can access the spreadsheet from the resource section (breakfreemoneybook.com/resources) to help you out. It has a list of typical expense categories that can get you thinking about what you spend in some main areas. Additionally, using something like Mint.com or a similar option is a great way to link all of your accounts and quickly get an idea of what you spend.

Whatever route you go, there are two considerations to keep in mind. First, you need to know what costs you have each month. Second, you should know what can be eliminated *and* what new expenses might occur (for a period of time) once you break free.

One positive "side effect" of this exercise is that you may find you don't need to make what you're making now to live the life you want, *especially* if you're building up an asset (your business) along the way! In a lot of cases, people that are making multiple six-figures find that it's more about meeting their lifestyle needs than it is about "replacing their income."

Not sure how much you need to really live the life you want? Check out Bonus #1 in the back of this book for a quick walkthrough. Even if you are already certain, it's worth a review because it might add some comfort knowing that you don't have to replace as much as you originally thought.

Let's break down your expenses now.

Step One

Either through a spreadsheet, pen and paper, or an app/website like Mint.com, add up all of your expenses so you know what you spend each month. You don't need to be perfect, and each month will differ somewhat, and that's OK. Get an idea of the average of the last few months and you'll be left with a reliable view of what you realistically need.

Step Two

Now that you have your list of expenses, you want to break them down into two categories: level one expenses and level two expenses.

Level one expenses are those that add value to you and your family and will remain once you break free. These are your "core" expenses that you really need to live and, in some cases, stay comfortable as a family. Often, these fall into some or all of the following categories:

- Housing (mortgage, rent, utilities, insurance, etc.)
- Food (groceries and reasonable eating out)
- Health care (paying for insurance, visits, medicine, etc.)
- Education costs (if you have kids or even for yourself)
- Transportation (vehicles, insurance, etc.)
- Pet care (since life is better with pets)
- Giving/charitable donations (if you give and plan to continue)
- Etc.

It can be intimidating adding up what you really need to spend, but remember that you (will) have a plan to offset those with income from day one of breaking free.

Level two expenses are ones that are nice to have but either will go away or *can* go away (for a period of time) when you leave employment and go out as self-employed. Keep in mind that you're looking at what you can cut out for a short period of time, not for the remainder of your life. Some examples of level two expenses might include:

- Excess eating out
- Subscriptions such as cable, magazines, etc.
- Big home projects
- Excess entertainment (movies, shopping, etc.)
- Updating wardrobes and other seasonal items
- Etc.

Anything you can plan to reduce temporarily increases and lengthens your financial runway and puts you in a safer, more secure spot when the time comes.

If you choose to "cut" some of these expenses, know that it is almost certainly temporary. The point is to enhance your financial situation for your transition so you have more "wiggle room" as you go about creating your dream business and life.

Step Three

After breaking down your level one and level two expenses, there's one more area to consider: what expenses might you end up having to add as you break free. Remember, this is about gaining awareness and the more aware you are, the better positioned you'll be to succeed. These potential additional expenses might include:

- Health insurance (especially if you go on COBRA, or extend your employer's insurance for a period of time)
- Startup costs (these can be minimal, but if you have licenses or other items, you'll want to factor them in)
- Subscriptions and resources for your new business (we'll break these down later, but include anything you know you'll need)
- Office space (or other physical location rent)
- Travel for work (potentially to establish new relationships or referral partners)
- Etc.

Expense Name	Annual Expense Value	Monthly Expense Value	Expense Level
Housing	$55,000.00	$4,583.33	1
Food	$10,000.00	$833.33	1
Health care	$6,000.00	$500.00	1
Eating out	$3,000.00	$250.00	2
Subscriptions	$500.00	$41.67	2
Entertainment	$6,000.00	$500.00	2
Kids care	$9,600.00	$800.00	1
Pets	$2,400.00	$200.00	1
Misc "stuff"	$6,000.00	$500.00	1

Taking your level one income (the income that will remain) and subtracting your level one expenses (your "core" expenses) gives you an important figure. In almost all cases, that number is negative since you have removed your current income from the calculation. *But,* that gives you a clear picture of what you need to cover each month, which is a critical step in laying out your financial runway (which is the next chapter).

Primary Cash Flow Trackers	
Current Total Monthly Income	$33,250.00
Current Total Monthly Expnses	$8,208.33
Current Total Monthly Net Income	**$25,041.67**

Summing Up Your Cash Flow

Getting clear on your cash flow is one of the most freeing things you can do financially and it's critical for being able to break free from your employment safely and successfully.

One of the benefits of this exercise is that you will generally know what you *really* need to live the life you want. I can list hundreds of cases where people making multiple six-figures (and even less) realized that they would be happy earning quite a bit less and using that free time to pursue other passions and build other businesses.

So, as you go through this, keep an eye out for what your "number" is - how much you really need to make each month to live the life you want! (And, again, check out the bonus section in the back for additional help).

Take a quick moment and appreciate that you now know your net worth, cash flow status, and exactly what you have available (assets) and what it takes to run your life (expenses) when you break free. Your core foundation is already built!

Next, you will learn how to enhance your "financial runway" that you've been seeing pop up throughout the book so far. In short, it tells you how long you can pay your bills without income. That's a critical step laying your solid financial foundation as you make the leap to self-employment.

CHAPTER

9

Determine And Extend Your "Financial Runway" So You Can Confidently Break Free

You've made it this far, which means you are committed to making your move to self-employment a success! You should now have a solid understanding of your net worth and cash flow. For most of us, the "money side of things" can serve as the single biggest holdup to taking the leap and being your own boss.

This chapter shows you how to smartly leverage your resources to ensure you're in the best possible financial position to break free by increasing the amount of time you can sustain your lifestyle once you leave your employment income behind.

First, you will develop a solid understanding of what your financial runway is and why it matters so much. Second, you'll calculate your financial runway as it stands today. Third, you will learn what to do if your runway feels "shorter" than you need. Fourth, you will discover ways to enhance and extend your runway. Fifth, and finally, you will establish a backup plan that allows you to go "all in" while still knowing you're being prudent on your journey.

➢ Your Financial Runway: What It Is And Why It Matters

Years ago, a Southwest Airlines 737 aircraft accidentally landed at the wrong airport in Wichita, Kansas with just enough runway for the plane to safely come to a stop. Everyone on board was safe and sound (although not where they thought they would be), but there was a problem: The runway at this particular airport was too short for the large plane to take back off.

Airplanes require longer distances to take off than they do to land. That meant the Southwest plane was stuck until it could be set up properly and the winds were favorable. Eventually, the pilots were able to safely take off and get the plane back into its normal rotation for the company, but not without additional risk, cost, and a hit to the confidence of the airline. For anyone looking to break free from their employment and launch their own venture, the situation illustrates a good lesson.

Before you start, make sure your "runway" is long enough to build the momentum you need to successfully take off and fly.

An aircraft needs a certain amount of distance given its size, weight, power, and outside factors such as winds, just as you will require financial assets sufficient enough to cover your expenses and give you the time needed to build momentum to successfully launch your new venture.

The length of your financial runway is simply a measure, in months, of how long you can survive without income from your current job based on your assets and expenses. Knowing how long it is now and taking steps to lengthen it will give you greater comfort (and a larger safety net) when you do break free.

It all starts with determining how long your financial runway is now.

➢ Calculating Your Financial Runway

Remember that phrase, "all progress starts by telling the truth," from Chapter 1? For our purposes, this means getting a clear and truthful picture of exactly how long your runway is now and what options you have to extend it. Even though you are designing your business to bring in revenue on "day one," it's still prudent to know where you stand and how to improve your current foundation so you don't "get stuck on the tarmac."

Calculating your financial runway is a quick process that gives you some really valuable information that will help you for your overall financial life, too. Feel free to use whichever method you prefer, and if you'd like a quick calculator tied into what you've done so far, download it at the resource site: (breakfreemoneybook.com/resources).

As with your other foundational pieces, we'll be breaking down your runway into two levels to simplify how you look at it. (And as before, "level one" is the runway you want to focus on, with "level two" serving as a back up mainly for reference only).

Level One Runway

Your level one runway is *your primary financial runway* because it's the one that doesn't unnecessarily subtract from your future financial well-being. It consists of your level one assets divided by your level one expenses (figures you calculated in Chapter 8), and is measured in months.

Financial Runway = Level One Assets / Level One Expenses = Number of Months You Can Afford to Pay Bills with No Income

As a reminder, your level one assets are those that are readily available to you now without penalty or major tax consequences, and your level one expenses are your "core" expenses that will hang around even after you leave your job. Put directly:

Financial Runway = Assets You Can Access Without Cost or Penalty / Expenses That Will Remain When You Leave Employment

The result of your financial runway formula is the number of months you can pay your current bills with *zero* income. That number paints a clear picture of where you stand and what's currently available.

A quick note: After you calculate your financial runway, you may be wondering, "Is that a good number?" You might also be saying to yourself, "That feels low." We'll tackle both of those in just a moment after we add up your level two runway.

Level Two Runway

Your level two runway gives you the "worst case" picture of how long you can live on your assets. It'll always be a larger number than your level one runway because you'll be including *all* of your assets that you can sell or cash out, if - and only if - you absolutely had to do so.

Level Two Financial Runway = Level Two Assets / Level One Expenses = Number of Months You Can Afford to Pay Bills with No Income

As you'll recall, your level two assets include all of your level one assets (those that can be easily accessed with no or minimal cost or penalty) *plus* the net assets you can access (but at a penalty or cost). "Net" in this case means what you would have after paying any taxes, fees, or penalties for accessing those level two assets.

If you don't know the cost or tax impact of using some of those additional assets, try multiplying their value by 0.65. This is the equivalent of a 35% "loss" to taxes or penalties if you were to use these assets. (As with all tax and legal items, you should consult your tax or legal advisor).

In almost all cases, tapping into these level two assets is *not* a good idea for your long-term financial well-being, so don't plan on using this runway. Having it handy, however, does show you that if things go wrong, you can extend your runway a little further to either (1) make things work or (2) go to your backup plan (discussed later in this chapter).

➢ What Is A Good Number?

How long should your financial runway be? That answer is different for everyone as it has a lot to do with how comfortable you are spending down assets, the speed with which you will bring in new income, how much income you need to replace, and how flexible your expenses are.

If you have a family or others depending on you, you're looking to replace a high income, or it takes a relatively long time for new customers/clients to decide to move forward with you, then you'll want a longer runway. In these cases, somewhere between eight months and a year is ideal. (If you don't have that yet, don't worry!)

If you're someone without too many obligations outside of yourself, such as no mortgage, no kids, etc., you aren't looking to replace a multiple six-figure income, and you have a short sales cycle with new customers/clients, then you can probably manage with a shorter runway of between three and six months (or maybe even less).

If you are designing your business, testing your offers, and being fully prepared on the day of your launch, you can take some of the pressure off of yourself with regards to the length of your financial runway. Still, the more runway you have, the safer you'll be (and feel) as you make the move to self-employment.

Having a long financial runway doesn't mean you have to spend it all either! It simply gives you more options to reinvest back into your business, pivot, or allows you to catch your breath at times. You'll never find someone who launched a business saying that he or she had too much "cash in the bank" or financial wiggle room!

As you think about the "right" number, ask yourself what you would feel most comfortable with and set that as a target. For example, if you sit back and say, "It can take a few months to get things going and I have kids, a mortgage, and I don't want to *ever* go back to my old job," then you may be better off having more runway (even if it means pushing your break free date out further).

There's no perfect number, and everyone eventually comes to two conclusions: (1) you'll always wish you had more, and (2) you can continue to lengthen your financial runway as you build your business. So, what if you feel like you don't have the length you need?

➢ What To Do If You (Feel Like You) Have A Short Runway

There are two components to this question. The first is "what if you're *really* short" on runway? This is different from "what if you *feel like* you're short even if you know you're probably OK?" Let's start with what to do if you really do have less than needed.

If you have less runway than you realistically need, you should spend the next weeks or months that you're building your business to also improve your financial foundation. As much as you may not like to hear it, it might also mean pushing your break free date out until you've reached your runway goal. When you make the leap, you need to do it in the right way and that means having a strong foundation to build on. Your financial runway is critical to your success.

What about if you're pretty sure you are in a good spot but you're still nervous or feel that you don't have enough? That's a tougher question, but there is an answer. If you're feeling that way, it could be because there are too many unknowns out there (How will I make money? How long will it take? Etc.). As you continue through the process of building out your business and putting a plan together (Chapter 11), you'll get answers to a lot of those "what ifs" and gain confidence in your position.

Regardless of where you are now or how you feel about your current situation, it's always a good idea to put effort toward extending your runway leading up to your launch.

➢ Lengthening Your Runway

The longer your runway, the safer your launch should be. That's because the number of months you can go without income coming in increases as your financial runway increases. Of course, you want to design things in a way that brings in income sooner rather than later, but any pilot will tell you they've never had too much runway! The same goes with your financial runway.

You can lengthen your financial runway by "pulling" one or more of four "levers" before you launch: (1) increasing your assets, (2) decreasing your expenses, (3) adding additional outside income, and (4) delaying your break free date.

If you increase your current assets and/or lower your current expenses, you will add to the number of months you are able to pay your bills once you walk away from your working income.

Likewise, if you increase your income, that will be less of a "drag" on your finances when you leave employment. As you might guess, delaying your launch date gives you more time to build your runway, leading to a longer timeframe to allow you to "take off." Below, we'll run through each of these one by one.

Increasing Assets Between Now And Launch

The first "lever" you can pull is to increase the amount of level one assets you have available to you before your transition to self-employed. Recall that your level one assets are the funds that are easily accessible without penalty or cost.

The most obvious option here is to save additional funds into a checking or savings account, keeping them in readily accessible cash. If you're spending less than you earn now, this should be easy enough. Simply store those funds in a way that you can access quickly as part of your launch. Don't worry as much about not earning interest or return on these assets, that's not the purpose here. The purpose is to remain accessible and increase your runway.

If you want to build an even greater "cushion," or you simply don't have a lot of "extra" at the end of each month, you could consider changing the location or account types in which you're saving funds. If you're contributing to a retirement account such as a 401(k) or an IRA, consider halting those contributions and, instead, place those dollars in a checking or savings account. Doing so gives you access to these funds without penalty (and potentially tax impact) and lengthens your runway because you now have freely available assets to support you.

In addition to these two savings-based options, consider tapping into some of the assets you already own, such as your 401(k) or permanent life insurance policy. (BIG NOTE here: this is not financial advice directed toward any one person, including you, and you should check with your advisor, insurance agent, or tax person. Both of these accounts can be easily ruined irrevocably if handled incorrectly, costing you to lose coverage, pay taxes, or experience penalties. It's your responsibility to do it properly.)

At the time of this writing, most employer-driven 401(k) plans (and also 403(b) and other qualified retirement plans) have a loan provision that may allow you to borrow up to half of the balance of the account, or $50,000, whichever is lower. One big caveat here: if you leave employment, that loan could be called in and you could be required to instantly pay it back or potentially be taxed on the amount still outstanding. Obviously, this is a potential problem if you're leaving that company. The good news is there is a solution that could also work for some.

You could open what's called a self-employed 401(k) or solo 401(k) as part of your "new job." So long as it's just you (and your spouse, if he or she will be joining or helping) working for your new business, you should be eligible to open one of these plans. A full explanation is beyond this book, so I would encourage you to do a little research or ask a trusted advisor.

Many providers offer these plans and they allow you to borrow from them. You will generally be expected to make payments back each quarter, but you're paying "interest" to yourself and, if done right, it's a tax-free way to access some of your retirement funds for launch. The key here being "if done right." So make sure you know the rules of your plan and are able to abide by them now and after you break free.

The same can be true if you have a permanent life insurance policy with cash value inside of it. (Just as with your retirement plans, you want to do this correctly, so make sure you talk to your insurance person to get the proper process, options, and guidance on how to do it.)

If you do have a "cash value life insurance policy," it's possible you can borrow - and potentially even withdraw (meaning you don't have to pay back) - some of that cash to lengthen your runway. This can be a great option for some people, but make sure you don't jeopardize your coverage if you need it!

Get Creative For Funding

One way to get additional funding for your business is simply to get creative. I'm not a huge fan of loans for starting a self-employed business, especially if you're doing more consulting, training, or service work because there is usually very low startup overhead and the loan has to be repaid regardless of the success of your business. Not only can that cause financial risk to your personal life, but it can add unneeded stress in the early days of self-employment. That being said, there are a few ways you can gain funds from others without the stress of "owing" anyone money.

Selling part of your future business for cash ("selling equity") usually isn't practical at this stage, because there likely isn't much value to the business yet. But that doesn't mean you can't come up with a similar "phantom equity" approach for family or someone you know that has excess funds they'd be willing to invest in you.

For example, let's say you need another $35,000 to have a secure runway. Instead of borrowing or selling part of your company (for which neither may be an option), offer 15% of all revenue (or whatever number) to the person who "gives" you the money until they've received $50,000 (or any amount you agree to) back. You can even structure it in different percentages at different revenue levels to work out a deal, and show them the plan you're building *and* your backup plan, so that they have greater comfort.

Think of this option as having the benefits of a loan without the risks. You only have an obligation to pay the funds back once you're successful (versus starting immediately) and you get to retain full ownership of your company. Of course, your reputation and character require you to give it "your all" and pay the investment - and gains - back as soon as possible, so make that a priority if this is the route you choose.

Part of being successful at the self-employment game is combining creativity with resourcefulness. Don't be afraid to get creative, and know there are always ways to lengthen your runway - even the ones you maybe haven't yet thought about!

Decreasing Expenses Between Now And Launch

One of the simplest ways to extend how long you can pay your bills with your level one assets is to reduce your expenses. You did some of this in the last chapter but it's worth another look here. If you prioritize your expenses, are there "nice to haves" and not "must haves" that you can cut for a short period of time while you build your business and launch? If so, consider doing it.

Take a moment and recall your Payment Pain ratio from Chapter 8. If you have a debt with a high Payment Pain ratio, it means that you pay out a lot monthly compared to the balance of the debt. (Causing you a lot of financial "pain" to carry this loan). If this is the case, it *may* make sense to take a level one asset and pay off that debt now to free up some assets to add length to your runway.

While you'll be reducing your assets to do this, you'll also be decreasing your expenses. Do a trial run first and recalculate your financial runway by removing the amount required from your level one assets and the expense associated with this debt. If your runway number - the number of months - goes up, using this option can lengthen your runway.

You can do this trial-and-error exercise for your financial runway for various scenarios, too. This can allow you to see how changing different variables will impact your results to help you choose what's right for you.

There are times when refinancing existing debt can be helpful as well. If, for example, you have balances on credit cards but a lot of equity in your home, you could consider a refinance of your existing mortgage. This can allow you to access cash to pay off those credit cards, which might lower your interest rate *and* significantly reduce your monthly payments. This happens because you would be changing short-term, high-interest debt into longer-term low-interest debt. In turn, this increases your financial runway. Even though your assets don't change, your expenses go down. For most this may not be the best option, but it's worth exploring everything on the table.

One positive aspect to consider about making the transition to self-employed after leaving a job is that your taxes and commute costs may drop temporarily, too. So as you "do the math" on reducing your expenses, also account for any costs that might decrease along with your income.

Use some creativity, out of the box thinking, and good advice from qualified and experienced people, and you'll be able to come up with some very doable solutions to extend your financial runway. (And that creativity and out of the box thinking will prime your brain for building your business, too!)

Adding Income Between Now And Launch

If you've explored increasing your level one assets and reducing your expenses and are still looking to extend your runway, consider adding other income. When you think of taking on another income stream, it could either be by you or someone else in your household.

When we talk about increasing your household income from someone other than you, it can be a slippery slope. For most of us, it can feel strange to ask a spouse or partner to look into adding some income by working harder or more hours to lengthen our runway. After all, having that person put more on his or her shoulders so we can pursue our dream doesn't always go over well!

That being said, the "ask" would be temporary, and as long as you're designing your business properly, the outcome would be a better life for all involved. Even if you don't want to ask them to put in more hours or pick up another job, see if the options mentioned previously with *their* 401(k) or life insurance might be available. One of the most overlooked strategies is a potential retirement plan loan from a spouse or partner remaining in a job. (Of course, all the same "seek advice" guidance and caveats mentioned above apply here, too).

This is also a good time to discuss these options with your family (or Family of Choice) as anything you do here can impact them as well. Sometimes, you'll be amazed at the support you can find!

For most people, any increase in income might come from doing extra work. Are there some part-time consulting opportunities in your current or future field? Would there be a chance to carry on as a part-time contractor with your existing company for a couple of months to help with the transition?

If the idea of sticking in your field, and especially your same company, doesn't fit the bill (you are breaking free, after all!), then there are plenty of other options for some extra income. Anything you do, though, be careful not to take up too much time or let it become a distraction from what you're *actually* doing - building your own business.

Adding Income - Pick Up A Part-Time Job

There's a very real chance that if you're focused on starting your business and are planning it out (which you are!), your time is better spent working on that and not a part-time job. That being said, you may not need a full 10 hours a day every day to work on your new business and, instead, can extend your runway by taking a part-time job. Try and find something in the field in which you'll be operating your business, or one that you might serve in your new business, so that you add expertise and knowledge to your skill set if you do take this route.

Adding Income - Do Some Not-Ideal Contracting Work

Depending on the work you do and the skills you inventoried, you may be able to do some contracting work. If it's different than the business you're starting, that can be OK. Remember, it's a temporary assignment to expand your financial runway so you can safely break free and be in control of your future when the time is right.

Adding Income - Create An Asset That Generates Income

This is where the "gold" is when it comes to adding income. You can create an asset that will benefit your business once you launch *while* bringing in some money before you do so. This could be a book that sells, an online course, or a consulting package. These are the "authority assets" described in detail in previous chapters, and they are incredibly powerful because they make you *the* authority in your space while potentially generating some additional positive cash flow in the now.

As with anything entrepreneurial, it's about balancing creativity and resourcefulness with focus. Adding income is a great idea as long as it doesn't distract away from building your business and taking the actions required to succeed. If you can balance it, however, it's an excellent way to lengthen your runway.

Delaying Your Break Free Launch Date

For a lot of people making the move to self-employment, there's a burning desire to "get out Dodge" as quickly as possible. If you don't have your financial runway quite where you want it or where it needs to be, then a delay might just be the prudent decision.

A delay isn't a full stop, but a temporary push back to more safely launch your business. Everything from product rollouts to space launches to the D-Day invasion have been pushed back for one reason or another, and two things occurred: (1) the pushback proved effective and, (2) no one remembers the slight delay, only the ultimate victory.

Use any time you delay to make your business better so that when you do launch you have a stronger offering for the market *and* more cash in the bank. It's not simply a time where you sit idly to let money pile up, but a time where you put in some extra work to make sure what you create is even better. Done right, lengthening your financial runway is a side benefit of the better company strategy with which you will launch.

➢ Establishing A Backup Plan

There's a chance you've heard some version of "give yourself no outs!" or "burn the ships![17]" when it comes to starting a new venture. In business, the parallel is not giving yourself an out, or a "Plan B," to fall back on.

Those are great rallying cries, but for most people, they are simply not practical. You can still go "all in" on your business and give it everything you have while having a plan for the worst case scenario. In fact, I believe it's reckless not to. There comes a point when you have enough obligations that having a backup plan is the best thing to do, if for no other reason, you never have to worry about "ruining" things for those that depend on you.

So, as you take this journey, it's up to you to determine what kind of backup plan you want to have. No matter what you're doing, know this: *you are marketable, have value, and can work your way into another job if you ever needed to.* Now, that's not the mission - and

17 "Burn the ships" is most often attributed to the 1519 invasion of Mexico by the Spanish. Their leader, Cortes, gave the order to "burn the ships" so that his troops had no other option but to win. While issues with history's events are out of scope here, the point of the quote is that giving yourself "no outs" isn't always smart. I would argue that it is better to have other avenues of success.

you'll have everything stacked in your favor by the time you're done here - but knowing that can help you feel more at ease as you go to launch.

Take a few minutes and write down the answer to the question below. Once you have done so, file it away and fully commit to the rest of this process.

The question: *If you run out of runway, for whatever reason, and you're not where you need to be, what will you do, even if it's not what you want?*

This may be a question to discuss with your family or anyone who will be affected by the answer, so make sure you all are on the same page. (Again, you may be surprised at how it feels with the extra support once you all are!)

This answer also doesn't mean that if you do have to go to "Plan B" that you have failed. It may simply mean that you need some more time to plan, regroup, and start again with what you learned the first time. *Never* settle for giving up your dream entirely!

➢ Summarizing Your Financial Runway

If there's one thing that you can do to better your long-term financial life and launch safely into self-employment, it's being totally clear (and truthful) on your financial runway and taking steps to extend it.

The good news is you can put many different things to work as you design and build your perfect business, meaning any actions you take now will be working for you before and as you launch.

You've come far! All that's left is making your business "ready to go" and putting some final, formal touches on it to keep you legal and on the right path. Once done with that, it's time to put it all together into a "playbook" that tells you what to do each day until launch to be a massive success.

CHAPTER

10

Making Your Business Official And Professional

This book has taken you through a process of identifying your most valuable skills, designing the right business, determining what you could uniquely offer, and getting your financial foundation and "runway" set. That's the order the process should follow, and I'm convinced you should do all of that *before* you start the formal aspects of setting up your business.

When the excitement of starting a new business kicks in, it's tempting to want to "play business" by setting up an LLC, ordering business cards, or designing a website. The problem with that approach is it feels like you're making progress when you're really just doing busy work before you know what service you will provide or how you will bring in revenue. Until you know exactly what you will be doing and how you will generate income, you don't have an actual business! (This is me speaking from experience, not passing judgment - we've all been there).

When you go in the correct order, however, getting all of the formalities out of the way aftward is actually quite easy. You simply need to know what it's going to cost to get off the ground, structure your business correctly, and take care of things like forming an entity (if necessary), handling the money and records, and deciding how to pay yourself. That's what this chapter covers for you.

Step one is figuring out what funds you should set aside to smoothly, safely, and cost-effectively launch your firm.

➢ What Will It Cost You To Get Off The Ground?

The reality is that just about any business will have some costs to get started, and yours is likely no different. The key is beginning with exactly what you need and nothing more, knowing that you can add on and scale up your expenses once you're generating revenue.

Here are a few general principles when it comes to figuring out what it will cost you to get off the ground. Once you have an idea of what you will need, you can map it out as part of your overall financial runway and launch strategy.

Be Thorough, But Stay Nimble

Keep your start-up expenses as minimal and as flexible as possible from the beginning. You can expand resources and open up your wallet a bit more once you're up and running. Early on, the name of the game is keeping your outflow as low as possible until you have consistent revenue coming in, even if that means adding in more "sweat equity" into the mix.

For example, if you require office space, instead of signing a three- or five-year agreement, rent out a room or office at a temporary location. It might be slightly more expensive for the months you use it, but you'll save yourself a headache and a lot of cost by not being tied to a longer term lease if something changes and you need to pivot.

Similarly, if you need to subscribe to software, periodicals, or other monthly resources, elect to pay month-to-month even if there's a savings for an annual subscription. While likely not the most cost-effective or efficient over the long-term, it is the most flexible, which minimizes your risks and gives you options in the early days.

The same goes for any staff. If you really do need help right out of the gate, consider finding some other self-employed people who would work as independent contractors ("1099s"). 1099 contractors simply require that you pay them only for the work they do, which gives you freedom from the cost of employees and ongoing pay/benefits[18]. Once you're successful and growing, employees are an excellent way to scale. (Although, you may want to keep things small and simple and limit your business to what you can do yourself or with the help of a virtual assistant or two).

Finally, don't forget insurance. It may not be the most enjoyable topic, but it is essential. The best place to start is with health insurance. Never go without health insurance, regardless of how tempting it might seem. The surest way to wreck your financial life is to not be insured when you need it. Most often, COBRA can be elected from your job when you leave, which should allow you to keep your plan for at least 18 months, although you most likely have to pay the full cost of the plan.

---

[18] This is another area where you should consult with your tax advisor. You don't want to be incorrect and think you have a 1099 relationship with someone while the IRS deems it an employer-employee relationship. That mistake can be costly, but there are good general rules to follow that an expert can help with.

Other options are the Healthcare.gov exchange, which can be costly if you don't receive subsidies, but reasonable if you do (which are based on your income). Detailed advice about health insurance options is beyond the scope of this book, but do seek out some professional help if you're unsure, as the above information is simply general guidance.

The other piece of insurance you'll absolutely want to consider is professional liability insurance, sometimes called "errors and omissions insurance." You will want to work with a good company to get this in place and to get proper advice. If you're doing a lot of consulting for your business, having this insurance can protect you (and your clients) if you accidentally give bad advice or make a mistake. Generally, it's reasonably priced for what it "does" and it's a great peace-of-mind investment for you and the people paying you.

(One note regarding professional liability and errors and omissions insurance: If you do business with only one or two companies, such as with an engineering consulting assignment, it may be possible to have the company you're contracting with assume all liability through your contract. This is more common than you might think, and is worth looking into if you're going to be consistent with a low number of firms).

Don't cut costs with insurance, but look to keep your other expense items to a minimum, opting for flexibility over the best long-term value. As you prepare to launch, look for areas you can build what you need through "sweat equity" - or effort - to keep expenses low, and take comfort knowing that any company you give money to now will gladly take more later if you need to extend or lock in longer contracts to gain better long-term value.

Build Your Brand

There is a lot that goes into a brand, and I am no expert on the design and visual side of it all. What I do focus on, however, is what *you* stand for and what you are *known* for in the marketplace. That's the branding that really matters. A beautiful website or fancy logo won't save you if you lose credibility in the eyes of your clients. Your reputation, values, and results serve as the best branding you can have.

That is good news when you're starting out because you get to determine the impression the market has of you and your work! There's no legacy or assumptions about your company or who you represent because you are starting fresh.

As you enter the market and begin serving clients, do whatever it takes to become known as the absolute best, without exception, in your field. Whatever you say you will do, do it, and do it ahead of schedule, giving more than expected. Over-communicate, be proactive, and leave nothing to chance.

If you become known as a reliable person of integrity, word will spread quickly. If, on the other hand, clients don't know what you're working on, when it'll be done, and if it'll be right, word will spread quickly, too. The bottom line: *be flawless in the execution of your work.* If you are, your brand will be one of your biggest assets.

While your focus should be on you and what you'll deliver, you do need a *simple* web presence. Don't fall into the trap of believing you need to have a website like the big firms. Use this as another differentiator that shows you're small, nimble, and reliable. In almost all cases, a simple (but polished), one-page website with a clear statement of what you believe, what you do because of that belief, and who you do it for should suffice. (And always make sure they have a way to contact you!)

Build Your Assets

An asset is something that you own and generates income for your business and, ultimately, you. Your brand and the service you provide can be an asset. If you create an authority book (hopefully you will!), it's an asset. It's the same with anything you create for your business. Your reputation and reliability are your biggest assets early on, so focus on building those. When you do, you'll often find that there are a few additional assets you can create along the way, like a list of interested buyers or digital products such as courses or explanation videos.

You can turn your authority content into assets that bring in clients and income for you easier than you might imagine. If you've been working on articles and blog posts, compile them into an authority book that shows how you're the expert in your space. Add in a few notes about your standard operating procedures (SOPs discussed below), and it will clearly show that you are different from the competition. Creating an "authority book" in this manner is one of the biggest assets you could develop, and it'll pay dividends for years to come. (Visit breakfreemoneybook.com/authoritybook for a free guide on how to do so).

Things like podcast appearances and videos you create serve as assets, too. Remember, an asset is anything that has the ability to make you money and provides value to your business. Once you have these, you can use them over and over to establish your authority.

Finally, don't forget about the information and data you collect through your funnels. Even though the sites themselves may not be major assets on their own, the emails and names you collect through them are. If you add up how much each client could pay you over time, you quickly see how a quality list of names can be of value to you and your business.

The best part about building "authority" assets is there is usually very little financial outlay to create them. There might be plenty of "sweat equity," but that's part of the game, and you can leverage these for years to come. One of the most valuable uses of our time as entrepreneurs is creating something once that can be delivered to clients (and generate income) many times and well into the future.

Hopefully, that gives you some quick tips on keeping costs low and building some useful, long-term assets through your own effort. Now, it's time to get down to the formal side of business and discuss creating "SOPs," entity setup, keeping records, planning for taxes, and how to balance taking income from your business while ensuring you retain sufficient funds to fuel your growth.

➢ Structuring Your Business And "SOPs"

One of the biggest financial benefits of building a business is that you have the opportunity to create an asset for your net worth. You certainly have the ability to earn more income self-employed than you do as an employee, but the big "return" comes from the value of your business (the asset), exclusive of you. *If you create it right.*

Odds are that your business will rely heavily on *you* in the beginning. In those days, if you're not there generating income and serving clients, it's possible the revenue stops. The key to changing that over time - and building up value in your company - is documenting your processes so you can scale up and train others. These are called your "Standard Operating Procedures," or SOPs for short.

For years I thought documenting and recording procedures was a waste of time when I could be using those minutes to serve clients, generate new business, or work on making my company better. When I joined a coaching program, that quickly changed. I realized that taking the time to do it had two benefits: (1) it created the foundation for me to eventually hire and scale my business, and (2) it would allow my business to run without me there all the time, which is critical to it being worth something.

Your SOPs essentially answer the question of "How do I deliver on my offer?" at every step of your process. Bedros Keuilian[19], one of my favorite people to follow, calls the completed list of these your "alien abduction manual." If you get taken away, someone else can plug right in and take over, completing the task with the same level of effectiveness as you would.

Don't let that intimidate you or sound like more than it is. You can build out a lot of the "fine detail" tasks as you go and the major categories you'll want in there likely fall into less than 15 or 20 topics. Invest the time now, before you start, to lay out the big tasks and services that you will perform for clients into your first round of SOPs. When you do, your business will be more effective and efficient, and your confidence and clients will thank you.

Documenting these steps forces you to think clearly about every process and task you perform along the way. It also gives you the opportunity to identify areas where you have gaps or missing structures in your process and fix those *before* you make the move to self-employment, which adds not only a level of safety but also comfort to your decision. How much better are you going to feel (and perform) when you know your business and process is sound as you approach your first several clients?

---

19 Bedros Keuilian is the founder of Fit Body Bootcamp (as well as other companies) and the author of a great book, *Man Up*. He also has many hours of valuable content on his YouTube channel that's worth checking out.

Early on you will have to overcome the views of some potential clients that you're not as capable as a larger company. We know this isn't true (and being more effective is often one of the main reasons we break free), but others may not. The best way to overcome this is to use your SOPs as a sales tool.

When you have your SOPs documented, you can say (and show) that all aspects of your business are thought through and planned out. Clients love to see this and it can give the (correct) impression that you are more buttoned up than even the biggest companies. When I launched one of my wealth management practices, clients quickly realized we "had our stuff together" when we did a quick run-through of all the areas we had accounted for in our SOPs. The best part is most "big" businesses that you'll compete against don't have these!

An extra benefit of having your SOPs mapped out is that they can go a long way to providing an outline for an "authority book." I can attribute the bulk of my recurring income to these authority books, and so can many others. A core step in your overall success is your SOPs, so take the time to put it all together!

➢ Formal Business Considerations

When it comes to the formal aspects of creating your business, there are four major items: (1) setting up the right entity structure, (2) keeping and understanding financial records and details, (3) planning for taxes, and (4) deciding how and when you'll take income out of the company.

Let's break each of these down below, with one caveat: this is neither legal nor financial advice. Especially when considering what type of entity to set up, or if you need one at all, seek out professional guidance. The below information is intended to be purely educational.

Entity Formation

An "entity" is simply the structure for your business. There is a wide range of possibilities, with the most popular options being sole-proprietor (no entity), partnership (no formal entity), LLC (limited liability company), S-Corp (subchapter S corporation), and C-Corp (what we traditionally think of as a "big" company).

Certain types of businesses in different states may have more unique structures. For the purposes of this section, we're going to focus on having no formal entity (either as a sole-proprietor or partnership), an LLC, and an S-Corp.

(Anytime you're dealing with entities, you should work with your tax advisor and attorney. The below is educational in nature only and may or may not be the correct choice for you personally).

No Formal Entity

You always have the option to have no formal entity structure for your business. Of course, that doesn't always mean it's the best choice, but it is one available to you.

Many self-employed people start out just using their name or a "DBA" (Doing Business As), which allows you to have a company name tied to you as a person. In a lot of cases, that works just fine, especially if it's a low-risk business and you have the right insurance in place.

If it's just you in your business and you have no formal entity, then you are considered a sole-proprietor. You typically have all of the same tax benefits as you would with an LLC, but potentially less protection (again, which can often be mitigated with insurance and smart business practices). If you plan to do consulting for just a few companies it is possible you can reduce your liability through your contract language by having the hiring firm accept any liability, too.

If it's you and another person without a formal entity, then you are usually considered a partnership. While you should always consult a professional for specific-to-you advice, in my opinion, there is very little benefit and a lot more risk with having a partnership without a formal entity attached. You can both be liable for each other's actions (or lack of actions), and that liability can reach beyond your business assets into your personal and family life.

For a lot of self-employed people without partners, remaining a sole-proprietor and bypassing setting up an LLC or other entity works just fine (assuming proper insurance and contracts are in place). That goes against what we often see and hear from "experts," largely because of a misconception with "tax benefits and protection" that comes from a formal entity.

LLC

LLCs, or limited liability companies, are perhaps the most popular structures for new businesses. I believe that's for three reasons. The first is that they are generally very easy to set up (usually in a matter of minutes, depending on the state) and operate with little "upkeep." The second reason is often some "limited liability" protection attached. Third, there's a whole industry revolving around helping people setting up LLCs.

From a liability standpoint, you'll want to consult with a professional to make sure you're clear on how your other assets are and aren't protected. While an LLC with a properly drawn up Operating Agreement (a document you should probably have that dictates the terms and ownership of the LLC) can provide some level of insulation for your personal assets, it's not a "free for all" or "anything goes." You can likely still be held personally liable for anything criminal or negligent, so it's not a substitute for proper business practices or insurance. (It's called a *limited* liability company, not a *zero* liability company, after all).

From a tax standpoint, LLCs typically allow the same self-employment-related deductions that you have as a sole-proprietor. The default for LLCs is to be taxed as a "partnership," which simply means that as long as the only owner is you (and/or your spouse if you file taxes jointly), the IRS can classify it as a "disregarded entity." That means all income and expenses flow through to your personal tax return, which can be a big advantage and save you from having to file an additional return for the business.

If you have an LLC with a non-spouse individual, it's likely you will still be classified as a partnership and have to file a partnership tax return each year. The tax liability should still pass through to each of you individually, in proportion to your ownership, but the IRS requires a "partnership return" be filed each year.

There is an option to elect your LLC to be taxed as an S-Corporation, and that does carry some taxation/long-term benefits and costs. Those are beyond the scope of this book, but know that starting with a "standard" LLC is often good enough for the vast majority of people. When you're running strong and doing well later, your accountant can guide you on any other "elections" (the IRS term for different structures).

S-Corp

An S-Corporation (typically called "S-Corp" for short) is, in most cases, treated as a "pass-through" entity like an LLC, which can simplify the tax filing process for you. The big difference with an S-Corp is that there are several more hurdles you need to complete to be "legit," from having meeting minutes to proper ownership structure, to determining a reasonable salary, and so on.

Generally, an S-Corp provides similar liability protection characteristics as an LLC, but it's best to talk those specifics over with a professional. Additionally, and as mentioned above, you can often have the operating simplicity of an LLC and some of the perceived tax benefits of an S-Corp by electing for your LLC to be taxed as an S-Corp. (It gets messy, doesn't it?) S-Corps can be good options for the right people and situation.

The Big Point On Selecting An Entity

The bottom line on selecting an entity is that it doesn't matter as much as you think it does (or as much as your buddy or the legal document company ads might suggest). What matters is having your business built properly, carrying the right insurance, and operating it with care and proper business practices.

In most cases, an LLC is a reliable option that carries low risk of "getting it wrong." When you start bringing in more cash, that's when you can hire someone to help you sort through more complex options. Remember, keep it simple and flexible, and you'll not only keep your costs down but also free up time to grow and run your business.

Whatever structure you go with, you'll likely find that every attorney and accountant advises you the same thing (and when that happens, it's time to listen up): *keep separate bank accounts for your business and never commingle those funds with personal funds.* If something goes wrong, it's going to be a lot easier to maintain limited liability if you can prove you treated it as an entity separate from your personal assets.

Financial Records And Tracking

Keeping good records of everything you have going in and out is critical when you're self-employed. Doing so is necessary to give you a clear picture of how you are doing financially *and* it can keep you out of trouble with the IRS and state tax departments.

What Records Should You Keep?

Anything flowing in or out of your business with a dollar sign attached to it should be recorded and maintained. That means every expense, all income, bills, subscriptions, tax payments, distributions to yourself, and so on.

Anytime you have an expense occur, such as purchasing something for your business, grabbing a meal with a client, or making a payment, record it while it's happening or immediately afterwards. While it's tempting to think "I'll remember it later," it's rare that it actually happens, so get it documented right away. Tracking expenses properly is what allows you the opportunity to deduct costs and reduce the taxes you may have to pay, so staying on top of it is the smart thing to do.

For income, you need to document the amount, date, and source of the income. This will help you match up your tax reporting later in the year and allow you to analyze how your business is doing (which we'll talk more about in a moment).

How To Track And Keep Records

The only wrong way, in my experience, to track your income and expenses is in your head! Pen and paper, as well as a spreadsheet, can work just fine if that's your style. Tapping into widely-used software (such as QuickBooks or many others) can make it easy for you.

The best system is the one that you'll use consistently. For me, I quickly learned that the only one I would use every time was software and app-based. One big advantage of the digital web- or phone-based apps is that it's usually quick and easy to run a variety of financial performance reports to see how you're doing.

Tracking And Reviewing Your Financial Performance

There's a saying that goes, "What gets measured gets managed."[20] The better you track your income and expenses, the easier it will be to make decisions and know what's working and what's not. You'll also be better equipped to know how much you can safely take out of your business versus leaving in for growth.

While in the early days of a new business, the immediate priority is often just generating income, long-term profitability tends to come from a constant awareness of what's coming in, going out, and what is left over each month. You'll be best served if you start recording those items from day one so that you have an accurate picture in the future. And, when you realize you're making it and pulling in cash a few months down the road, it's a great experience to look back and see how far you've come!

Using any of the well-known software or app-based record-keeping systems makes it easy as they have quick reports that show how your money is flowing through, what you're making net of expenses, and how the assets of your business are stacking up.

---

[20] I *believe* this originated with the management guru, Peter Drucker. It's been used frequently and modified in many different ways over the years.

I've laid out what I believe are the three most important financial metrics below to track as you get started. Before that, know that where you start isn't where you'll end. Don't get in the trap of thinking the numbers won't "look good" now just because you're in the beginning stages. (It would be surprising if they did). Instead, it's about awareness. Those who are aware of their situation tend to outperform (usually significantly) those who aren't.

Metric To Track: Income Vs. Expenses

When you have more money coming in than going out, you're making money. Even though being self-employed can provide freedom and more fulfillment than working for someone else, your main function is to generate sufficient net income to cover your lifestyle and family needs.

By tracking your income and expenses, you know what your different margins are. Having "margin" means your business is bringing in a greater amount of money than you are spending to acquire business and provide services. That "gap" is the key to building significant wealth, and that means it's something you want to track.

Metric To Track: Total Cash

If you could watch one measure over time to give you an idea of how your business is doing, it would be the balance you have in cash. The timing of payments and money coming in can impact this in the short-term, but in the long-term, what's "sitting in the bank" doesn't lie. It's also one of the simplest and easiest measures to track.

Seeing your cash accumulate after transitioning to self-employed is an incredible feeling and sets the stage for you to start "paying yourself" by taking money out of the business. As this balance goes up, your ability to fund your lifestyle and do all the things you want to do for yourself and your family increases as well. It's a powerful indicator to watch.

Metric To Track: Balance Sheet (The Net Worth Of Your Business)

Always track the "worth" of your business. To me, this is different than the value of your company, because it excludes what is arguably your most important asset at this point: *you*. The net worth of your business is all of the assets that fall under it (such as cash, savings, authority content, equipment, dollars people owe your company, etc.) minus any debts you have (what you owe others, loans, taxes you know you'll pay, etc.).

Tracking the net worth of your company lets you see that, not only are you generating an income for yourself and your family, but you're also building an asset that increases your personal worth! Since you own your business, it flows through to your family "balance sheet" and increases your net worth. This is where the *real* wealth in self-employment comes from, so track it diligently.

Planning For Taxes

(A friendly reminder that with anything financial or legal, you should consult a professional. The below is not to be taken as advice for you, and is only educational with the goal of giving you a few "guidelines" to begin your planning).

A mentor of mine (from afar) in the financial planning world, Ron Blue, always said that "Taxes are symptomatic of income," meaning that if we're paying more in tax, it's because we're making more money. I always try to keep that in mind when it comes time to pay up each quarter because the "sting" of taxes is real.

When it comes to running the financial side of your business, taxes aren't something to mess around with. Get a good tax professional to help minimize what you can within the context of the law and then pay what you owe on time.

It can be tricky knowing what to pay early on because you don't know how your year will end up. The total amount due is also impacted by your other income (if you were employed in the same year, and perhaps a spouse's earnings) and, of course, what you come out with on the "net" after expenses at the end of the year. Unfortunately, the IRS doesn't care or give you much grace here.

Because of that, it's best to be proactive and do two things: (1) plan your pricing and expenses to account for ~1/3rd of your income going towards taxes, and (2) set aside a portion of each "check" you receive so you have funds ready to go to cover the potential taxes.

Planning on 1/3rd of your inflows going to taxes may sound high, and it very well could be after you deduct expenses, but it will guide you on charging enough to give yourself a little breathing room. Then, come tax time, if you have some left over, enjoy it or use it to reduce the next round.

In general, you're going to want to make what the IRS calls "estimated tax payments" four times a year, with an additional "square up" payment if you owe additional money at tax time, usually mid-April. This means you need to plan your cash flow to have sufficient funds available every few months to pay the IRS and your state (if your state has an income tax).

There's a lot more to the tax picture, but hiring a good tax professional usually pays for itself a few times over.

Balancing Taking Income And Leaving Money In The Business

Once you've set aside what you need for taxes and are tracking your cash balances, business worth, and income and expenses, you should have a good idea of what's left at the end of each month. Once you're consistently bringing in more than you need each month, it's likely time to consider taking money out of your business to pay yourself for all the work you're doing!

You may be focused on survival and keeping your financial health strong in your first several months. During that time, you'll likely plan to pull more money out of your business to pay living expenses and that's acceptable, and possibly even wise. You will get to the point where you have extra cash beyond what you need to live and have the decision of leaving it in the business to help further growth or taking it out and either spending it or investing it on your personal side.

Deciding which is best depends on a handful of factors, and there are a few questions I like to ask myself before choosing the best course of action.

Question One - Do I Need This Money To Fund My Living?

Simply put, if you need the cash your business is generating to live off of, then the right decision is likely to pull it out. This is common in the early days as you look to replace your employment income. It's usually safe to do, with a couple of caveats: (1) make sure you have funds to pay taxes and bills later, if needed, and (2) be aware that it could reduce the amount of growth your business has in the future if "cash now" could be used to accelerate future sales instead of being taken out of the business.

If you're running your business pretty "thin" and you aren't generating a large amount of income after expenses, you may not need to set aside quite as much for taxes in the beginning. And, if you're growing over time, there will be plenty of opportunities to reinvest for the future later on.

Bottom line: if you need the cash from your business to live off of as you launch, do it! That's what it's there for and as long as you keep at it, you'll have the growth you need.

Question Two - If I Leave It In The Business, How Will I Leverage It?

When your business is generating more than you need to live off of, the name of the game becomes identifying the most productive thing to do with those funds. If you know putting that money to work in your company will help you grow and generate more income or value in the business itself, it's a good decision to leave it and make those investments.

If you don't know what you'd do to expand your business with the excess funds, you're probably better off pulling them out and putting them toward a productive use on your personal side. This could be anything from paying down debt to investing in a self-employed 401(k) or other retirement plan, or simply building up assets for your family.

This is a good problem to have, and one that you'll eventually face if you keep at it!

Question Three - If I Don't Need It And Don't Leave It In The Business, What Will I Do With It?

If you don't need the money for living expenses and you're not going to leave it in the business, what should you do with it?

The short answer is *use that extra cash to build your personal net worth.* When you purchase assets or invest in things likely to appreciate over time (such as stocks, real estate, or other appropriate investments), you're creating legacy wealth for your family, and that's what this is all about.

Stay consistent with everything you've designed and built so far and you'll work your way to the point where your business is providing more than enough for you. Whether you choose to use those funds to scale and grow or to simply live a better life, you get to be the one to decide. *That* is how you start controlling your destiny.

➤ Summarizing Making Your Business Official

Getting the formal and financial considerations right for your business is important, but should happen in the right order (*after* you have an actual business mapped out). Set aside what you need to launch, understand the entity structure required, and track and have a plan for the dollars coming in and going out.

When you have that lined up, you're ready to put *all* of this together into a simple plan with every step you need to take. You really *are* that close, and that's what we're going to tackle next.

PART 3

Putting It All Together In A Plan And Taking Action

CHAPTER

11

How To Bundle Everything You've Created So Far Into A Plan For Success

In over 17 years of helping people plan and manage their businesses, money, and investments, I've consistently seen that those with a plan do better than those without a plan. I truly believe that constructing a *real* plan for your launch is the one thing that will dramatically increase your odds of success *and* safety for your family.

Planning is powerful. It's what separates those who win long-term from those who "wing it" and often have to retreat back to employment, depend on others, or face more stress than needed.

There are plenty of misconceptions about what a "plan" is and what the process means. In the simplest sense, planning is an exercise that takes you from a clear "Point A" to a definite "Point B" as efficiently as possible while reducing the number of decisions you'll have to make "on the fly."

The goal of the planning process is to leave you with a playbook for your launch. Much like elite sports teams have definite plays that they run to accomplish certain outcomes, newly created businesses should, too. That's what this chapter is about: how to simply, easily, and effectively create your plan and playbook based on what you've already laid out and designed.

We'll start by making sure we have a firm grasp on what planning is and isn't.

➤ The Basics Of Planning

Ask any successful business owner or high-net worth individual if he or she spends time planning his or her personal and professional life, and you'll almost certainly hear "yes." Many of these individuals go so far as to create a plan for each and every day. If the people who are successfully running their own businesses and have a great deal of wealth do something consistently, it's something we should all strongly consider. Especially if we want to "be in their shoes."

What Is Planning?

Planning is an act that determines the steps and decisions required to reach an end goal. The outcome of this process is a *plan.*

I define a plan as *a prioritized and sequenced series of clear and definite actions that, when executed, delivers a tangible desired outcome.* Here's how that works.

If you're trying to get from "A" to "B," you need to know what each step is and the initial actions you should take. Each action or task needs to be sequenced - put in order of when you will accomplish it - so that all of the pieces of your plan fall together like dominos. If you maintain your predetermined order and don't skip steps, your likelihood of success increases because you will remain on the path needed to reach your end goal.

Effective planning also reduces the mental load that comes from having to make decisions in the future. The more we can plan the paths and actions we will take now, the fewer decisions we have to make in the future when we're in the thick of it and the stakes are higher. This gives us more time and mental energy to spend on actually taking action and accomplishing our goals (versus debating and deciding).

For all the things planning does, it's only part of the equation. Nothing is guaranteed, even if you have a plan, but your odds of success are dramatically improved. *Especially* if you're willing to put in the work and pivot or adapt as needed.

What Planning Isn't

Planning isn't magic. It can't make something happen that you don't put in motion. It's also not a guarantee, and a plan will only work *if you work it.*

You can have the most well-built plan in the world, but if it just sits in a Word document or a Google Sheets page, it's useless. The biggest mistake I see people make is putting together a very good plan, but then not actually *implementing* it. Planning isn't the end, it's the beginning. It's designed to tell you what to do and when, not something that runs on autopilot.

Planning also isn't static. While you should take the time to build a well-thought out and thorough plan, you must be willing to add to it and update it along the way. You can do that now by mapping out multiple options and "what ifs" for a variety of future scenarios, or you can simply be willing to pivot later on. Either way, you'll have the framework to adjust and adapt your plan as things change.

With all that said, should you put serious effort into planning?

Absolutely!

Planning is worth it, and it's the one thing that can bring everything together for your launch. In fact, much of what you've been doing up until now is getting the pieces together for your new venture. Now, to convert that to an effective plan, all you have to do is put those pieces in a *prioritized and sequenced order.*

Winning in business often happens at the margin. That means that it's the series of "little things" stacking on top of each other that brings ultimate success. Rarely is it "one big thing" that determines how successful you are. Planning is the key to identifying all of those small items in advance and putting them together in a way that stacks the odds far more in your favor.

This doesn't have to be difficult at all. Simple plans tend to be the easiest to follow and implement, and that's why I stick to simple (and recommend the same for you). Simple is fast, clear, easy, and rewarding.

➢ The Simple-But-Effective Planning Process

I use a seven-step planning process for many aspects of my life and those of my clients. I've found that breaking things down to that level not only allows for faster outcomes, but also ensures that the little things don't get missed.

Step One - Clearly Define Your "B"

GPS units and navigation apps need a clear destination to effectively plan out a route. You need the same idea when you're building your plan: a very defined destination or objective. I call that your "Point B" (as in "going from A to B").

Having total clarity on your "B" means knowing exactly what you want to accomplish. If it's a financial goal, you need the exact dollar amount. "Successfully launching my business" is too vague. So is, "Replacing my employment income with self-employed income." What does that success mean to you, and how would you quantify it?

Let's say you need $10,000 a month to live your life and care for your family and you want that to be your target goal, net of expenses, as you transition to self-employment. For the sake of this example, to get a *net* $10,000 into your personal account, let's assume you need to bring in $15,000 to cover taxes and your expenses. In this case, $15,000 a month of revenue generated by your business is a clear "B."

The next question is, "When do you want to accomplish it by?"

Step Two - Identify Your Deadline

Once you have a clear target, decide on when you intend to hit it. Take the time here to come up with a realistic timeframe, which may or may not be longer than what you *want*. Using the example above, you may want to be at $15,000 of revenue in your business by month two, but if you step back and look at it realistically, you may find that it requires a longer ramp-up to reach that goal.

This isn't to say that you shouldn't push yourself or try to accomplish your goals quickly. Of course, all else being equal, you want to be on and stay ahead of schedule. Remember, though, we're building your plan here - the daily tasks that go together to reach your goal - and the totality of those tasks need to be achievable in relation to your timeframe.

To continue our example, let's say you decide your goal is to have $15,000 of revenue coming in by month five in your business. If that's the case, you may want to generate business and "sign up" some clients in your first month, be collecting $5,000 worth of revenue by your second month, and have $10,000 brought in by your fourth month. (And then the $15,000 coming in by the end of month five). This gives you your target and also a timeframe with checkpoints along the way, then next you will need to identify the actions required to achieve both.

Step Three - What Needs To Be True To Accomplish Your Goal?

Remember the power of asking, "What needs to be true" from before? It's one of the most powerful and revealing questions you can ask as you go through the planning process while building your business. In our example, ask, "What needs to be true for me to be earning $15,000 in revenue in my fifth month of operation?"

The benefit of asking this question is it sends you down "rabbit holes" for each initial list item you come up with. For each of the things you list out, ask, "What needs to be true for that to happen?" Continue to do that until you have very definite actions listed.

When you first begin to leverage this question, it can be daunting because it may feel like you continue to uncover new items but few answers. *That is by design and a good thing.* Here's why.

Those "rabbit holes," or seemingly unending items, are going to come up whether it's now or in the future, and it's better to know what you need *before* you actually need it. You may not have all of the answers right now, and that's OK (and part of the process). You'll get those in the next two steps.

For now, start to list out all of the things that need to be true for you to accomplish your goal. Using our ongoing example, let's ask the question, "What needs to be true to have $15,000 of revenue coming in during your fifth month of operation?" Depending on your business and types of clients, the first item could look something like this:

Three signed and paid contracts (assuming each client pays $5,000 and 3 x $5,000 = $15,000 in this example).

Once you have that, ask, "*What needs to be true to have three signed and paid contracts in month five?*" The beginning of your next list might be:

- Contracts drawn up
- A way to collect the money
- Three new clients in the pipeline
- Your service ready to deliver
- Etc.

Looking at this list, we'd take each item and, as you might guess, ask, "What needs to be true for me to have contracts drawn up?" and so on. In the case of the contracts, we might answer: *Hire an attorney*. To hire an attorney to draw up the contracts, it's true that we'll need to *research and select the right attorney to partner with*. That becomes an action step.

When you get to where you have a concrete action (and the end of the "what needs to be true..." line of questioning), add that to a separate list to track, which I call your "Master Actions List." We'll come back to that in another couple of steps.

Simply repeat this for all of the items you come up with and you'll find you have a series of concrete actions to take that will move you forward. It may *seem like* there will be thousands of things to do, but you will quickly discover that not everything has numerous trails to run down, and many actions you list out will end up negating or automatically accomplishing others.

It's likely you'll find that you don't have all of the answers and resources you need as you build your Master Actions List. I refer to those missing pieces as "gaps." Those gaps need to be identified and filled, and that's the next step.

Step Four - Identify Any Gaps

You will identify "gaps" as you put your action items list together. These could be lacking an asset (such as cash in the bank, an authority book, equipment, etc.), knowledge, skills, tools, connections, or something else. That's normal, and it's *much* better to identify them now so you can address them proactively (versus finding out you have a missing piece later on when it's too late).

Once you have your list of gaps, simply ask yourself, "What do I need to do to close that gap?" (Notice it's simply a variation of the "What needs to be true?" question we've been using, only this time, it's putting it all in your control).

Using the ongoing $15,000 a month of revenue example, if you find you don't know if you have enough potential people to reach out to in order to have three new paying clients we identified as a need, ask, "What needs to be true for me to have more people to reach out to?"

List out the answers you come up with. In this case, we might create the following options/solutions:

- Start a referral partner relationship with someone who has those clients
- Identify Facebook and LinkedIn groups where the ideal market converses or "hangs out"
- Get an article leading to a funnel going in a trade publication
- Buy into mastermind groups
- Etc.

Then break down each option until you get concrete actions you can take. To start a referral partner relationship, for example, we might need to: *(1) identify the right potential partners, (2) approach them with an offer, (3) decide on the revenue sharing/financial arrangement, (4) agree to the relationship, (5) deliver on the relationship.* When you have those items, you can add them to your Master Action List that you began in step three. If you find that you need to add more tasks to fulfill each of those, add those to the list. Remember, it's much better to find this out now than when you're full speed ahead and on a deadline later!

Step Five - Prioritize Your Master Actions List

Between steps three ("What has to be true for this to happen?") and four (identifying gaps), you should have created a list of initial actions that will move you toward your clear "B" end goal. Some of those actions may be more concrete than others. Don't worry about the ones that aren't concrete yet; what's important is making sure you have as complete of a "Master Actions List" as possible at this point.

Once you do, it's time to prioritize those actions based on four different criteria. This part is a bit of an art as well as science, so know that there is no right answer and you can adjust and adapt as you go forward.

This part is what ties everything together, so please don't skip it! (Remember, a plan is a *prioritized* and sequenced series of clear and definite actions that, when executed, delivers a tangible desired outcome).

To rank the items on your Master Actions List by priority, evaluate for criteria related to each task: (1) the total time needed, (2) the impact of completing the action, (3) the ease of taking it, and (4) your current capacity to readily execute that task.

Criteria One - Total Time Needed

If you have a task that's going to take some time to work out, consider adding it early on in your priority list. A good example of this was our hypothetical "*research and select an attorney to draw up the contracts*" action above. This task can take time as it might involve initial searching followed by conversations and, eventually, selection of the right counsel. Whenever you have a task like this that will take a while to complete, set it earlier on in your sequence so you have the time to make progress.

This is especially true if you have an action that must be completed before other actions can be taken. Continuing our example, since you can't have a contract signed by a paying client before it's drawn up by the attorney you're selecting, you want to start that process sooner and, therefore, place it early in your plan.

Criteria Two - Impact Resulting From Completion

We are all creatures of momentum and there's something to be said for stacking up big wins. If you have a task that's a critical "lever" on your path to success, consider prioritizing it ahead of others. Big wins that move the needle have a magnifying effect over time (both emotionally and in reality), which makes them valuable to lead with.

Of course, not every task can go first, so you do have to balance out the actions that have a big (or lasting) impact with the other criteria and considerations. Oftentimes you'll find a task that other tasks will depend on, that is also easy to do, and would be a "big win." That is the trifecta for an early-to-complete task!

Criteria Three - Overall Ease Of Effort

Sometimes knocking a few tasks off of a big list feels good *and* moves you closer to your goal. Quick wins motivate us to keep going. When you run across tasks that are easy to complete (or take very little time), consider sprinkling some of those early on in your order of items to complete.

Don't shift more challenging tasks to later in the list if other things depend on them just to get a few easy ones up front. Instead, stack the easy ones in between and after these time-sensitive tasks, knowing you have a few simple ones that follow. That will balance boosting motivation and ensuring you stay on track.

Criteria Four - Current Capacity To Readily Execute

As mentioned previously, you'll find some tasks that have "gaps" requiring additional resources, knowledge, skills, connections, etc. Those are appropriate tasks to place earlier in the sequence so that you have the resources you need when you need them.

The point of creating your prioritized actions list is so that you have a sequence of tasks that you complete in a certain order. For each of these items, consider how long it might take you to complete. This is a good "FYI" number to keep in your head, and some people even like to block out the expected time required along with the tasks as part of the next step. It's my favorite step because it takes all of the guesswork out of when you'll accomplish each action!

Step Six - Schedule Your Actions

This step is what I believe separates the people that succeed with their plan from those who don't. I will tell you that all of the highly-successful business owners and wealthy people I know live by their calendars. If something is on the calendar, it gets done. If it isn't, it is very unlikely that it will (usually on purpose). It took me a *lot* of years (way too many) to embrace this habit, and it's the single best thing I've done for achieving goals and executing plans.

It's time for you to stack the odds in your favor by *taking each of your actions that you now have prioritized and schedule time on your calendar for every single one of them.* I would recommend placing the next 30 days worth of actions on the calendar to start, and then schedule a time toward the end of that timeframe to set the following 30 days of tasks. (If you work better in shorter time frames, consider doing the same thing but one week at a time versus 30 days).

The "balance" is ensuring you get enough tasks on the schedule to stay on track for your timeframe target while making sure you don't overcommit and get bogged down or overwhelmed. If you're going to err on one side or the other, err on the side of stacking your calendar a little lighter than you think you can do. That way, as you knock out the tasks, you'll be able to jump ahead (and enjoy the feeling that comes with doing so). You can always do more than what you have on your schedule!

This step takes time and work, but it will pay off in multiples down the road in both time saved and results. Finally, there's one more step in the planning process that keeps you on track and moving forward after you've scheduled your tasks: debriefing and adjusting.

Step Seven - Debrief And Adjust[21]

Each day take five minutes and review the tasks you completed and see how they have moved you further along your plan toward your ultimate goal. As part of this, ask the following question:

- *What worked well for accomplishing my tasks today?*
- *What can I get better at when it comes to accomplishing my tasks?*
- *Am I on or ahead of schedule? (If not, what can I do to get ahead of schedule?)*
- *What resources do I need to line up for tasks in the near future?*
- *What tasks do I have scheduled for tomorrow, and do I have what I need to successfully accomplish those?*

Going through these five questions each day will help you make progress *and* make you better at taking action and accomplishing your goals. When you go through the debrief each evening, *never* beat yourself up if you miss something. There's always room for improvement and tomorrow is a new day. Being in charge of your future and launching a successful business is a journey, and no journey is perfect!

---

[21] I first learned a structured way for debriefing from a good friend and pilot, Jeff Bonner. He has a process called "The Daily Debrief" that he's adapted from his time in military and civilian aviation. That's been invaluable to me in my personal and professional life.

When you do find some changes you can make for the better, implement them! Even if they are small, put them to work for you. Adjusting is the name of the game, as no plan stays static. Life and business move fast and you need to be ready to pivot and adapt your plan as required. The power of the debrief is that it allows you to catch and implement those opportunities quickly so you get, and stay, on track.

➤ Summarizing Creating A Plan

Hopefully, you see that planning is powerful and doable. It's what the most successful self-employed people do, and it is a common thread among the highest net worth people on the planet.

Planning is also a way to increase your own chances and magnitude of success while allowing you to spend more time on execution and taking action. It's a strategy that, by making decisions and setting tasks ahead of time, provides the opportunity to operate with a clearer mind. It's the key to going through each day with confidence because you know you're not just "winging it."

When you stack all of the benefits of planning together, and you use everything you've designed and created thus far, you're able to truly build a systematic way to accomplish your goals and get from "Point A" to "Point B" in your business.

Now that you have your business designed around *you*, and all of the specifics created and placed together in a plan with scheduled daily tasks, you are ready for one thing: *action*. It's time to make it happen!

CHAPTER

12

What Happens Now? (How To Win And Not Let Anything Stop You)

Only a small percentage of people who start reading a book finish it, and an even smaller percentage take action on what they've learned. If you're in the group that's made it here and started putting your break free plan together, congratulations!

You're not far off from the incredible world of running your own business and taking back control of your life. Take comfort knowing that you are putting in the work and have done what's needed to stack the odds in your favor and succeed. You may even be feeling the "high" that comes with making such progress. Now, there is only one step left: *implementing.* You have to act and bring your dream of self-employment to life.

Once you begin to take action, human nature is likely to kick in and cause you to face some hesitation and self-doubt. If that happens, *it's completely normal* to second guess yourself and wonder if your plan will *really* work. You might even run into others, including your closest friends and family, that tell you you're crazy for even having the idea. Fear might try to take over, but all of that is temporary and easy to overcome with the correct mindset and "input."

The good news is that once you openly acknowledge the presence of self-doubt, naysayers (even those coming from a place of love), and fear, you can take steps to move past these holdups. The *millions* of successfully self-employed people who have gone before you have done it, and now it's your turn!

So, in our last chapter together, let's address that head on and discover some ways to overcome those potential obstacles with the confidence and certainty you need to make the leap and start your next (and best yet) chapter.

As I've learned the hard way, burying our "heads in the sand" doesn't pay off, but acknowledging these issues and tackling them truly does!

➢ What Holds Us Back From Taking Action (And Why This Time Is Different)

I mentioned in the opening pages that I've had plenty of "false starts" over the years when it's come to taking action. That led me to seek out *why* it was that I often wouldn't execute, even when I had a good plan in place. What I learned through myself and others is that there are a few tweaks that can help overcome hurdles that result in inaction. Let's talk about some of the main ones.

➢ Fear Is A Liar

The most common reason humans don't take action on something they know can work is *fear*. It could be a fear of failure, or even of success and how it might change our lives. It may be a fear of judgment from others, perhaps particularly from those closest to us. The biggest fear, however, tends to be the *fear of making the wrong decision* and it costing us "everything." The good news is that's almost certainly not the case!

I've learned two interesting things about fear. First, it's not "real" in the traditional sense. Think about it: we've never *seen* fear, and have never touched it. Because fear isn't a physical object in the world, as soon as we realize that it *only* exists "between our ears," we recognize that we can defeat it.

The second thing about fear is that it is closely tied to doubt. It's only when we are unsure of our ability to accomplish something that we begin to fear it. If we have total confidence in our skill set or experience, we tend to not have fear. Take the example of walking down the stairs. Odds are, you don't fear that anymore because you've done it tens of thousands of times successfully (and even when you have fallen you came out fine). If it's something you've never done before, such as starting a business, then you may doubt your abilities.

There are ways to overcome that fear, and you will do so with the correct mindset. Know that it's natural to have doubts and be fearful of making a big transition. Truthfully, if you don't have at least some fear along the way it might be a red flag! Fear makes you aware of potential risks and opportunities that, if acknowledged and addressed, can be mitigated and managed so as not to stand in the way of your success.

Overcoming Fear

Years ago I heard that fear was best used as a "compass" pointing you toward exactly what you are supposed to do[22]. It sounded strange at

---

22 I *believe* I first heard this from Zig Ziglar content.

first, but since then, I've come to believe it and embrace it. Any time I feel a hesitation, I take a step back and realize it's probably pointing me in the direction of what I really should do.

For example, if I'm fearful about speaking on a stage, that's a good indication that I should probably do it. By deciding to charge head-first (prepared of course) into speaking, I'll be better for doing it once done. If I'm fearful of resigning from my job to start my own business, that's probably a sign that it's the next best move for me.

There are a few tactical things you can do beyond using fear as a compass to overcome it. Oftentimes it's a combination of the below strategies that gets you over the hump. All we really have to do is take the first step and momentum will take over and get us moving in the right direction.

Find A Bigger Fear

The idea of replacing whatever you fear with a bigger fear may sound strange at first, but it works. There's always a larger fear that's worse than the one holding you back. If you're feeling fearful about starting your business, ask yourself what else would be even more terrifying?

When I did this exercise, I came up with a two-part answer to the "bigger fear:" (1) staying forever where I knew I would continue to be unfulfilled each day, and (2) feeling like a failure to my kids because "dad" never took a chance to show them what's possible. Both of those were far scarier to me than the fear of leaving my job.

Those two greater fears made the idea of jumping into the "scary" world of self-employment feel less risky than the alternative of staying put. I realized that if I mapped everything out correctly and followed my plan, I'd have a good chance of succeeding. And, if it all went bust, I knew I could either pivot or rebuild what I had at a new job. While I didn't want to fail and take another job, it quickly shifted the risk-reward equation far enough in my head to hit "go."

Take some time and think of what would be worse than making the leap and coming up short. What would be even more terrifying to you? Is it staying where you are forever building someone else's fortune? Missing out on your potential? Dying early knowing you didn't give it a full effort? Letting your kids down? The goal isn't to go negative here, it's to put it all into perspective for you.

Plan What You Can

This one should be obvious by now - plan out every element and cover every variable that you can about your launch. For each unknown you remove from consideration, you reduce your level of fear. Map out what you can and you'll decrease your uncertainty enough to overcome the fear and go.

Take some time and build a plan for everything you can. Once you've done it, you'll be surprised at how much less stressful the move to self-employment looks. Planning stacks the odds in your favor and removes unknowns and variables, and *that's* what will beat back fear.

Write Out The Worst Case Scenario

Take a minute and write out the worst possible thing that can happen if you fail. Would you have to live with your failure, or go back to a job? Would you burn through all of your savings? Could you lose your house? Would your marriage dissolve?

None of those scenarios are good, and none of them should be minimized. Reviewing them adds perspective, though. While negative, they likely won't kill you (as a mentor of mine says), so take comfortking knowing you can "fix" just about anything that could happen. Most importantly, now that you know what the worst case scenarios might be, take the steps you can to avoid these issues in the first place (such as building your business correctly, planning out your move, getting your significant other on the same page, and enhancing your financial runway). That in and of itself will reduce your risk of a negative outcome.

Whatever the worst case is for you, come up with several ideas of how you can prevent it or lessen it dramatically[23]. When you designed your business you created a backup plan, so you're already part of the way there!

Letting Go

If you've done everything you can, then you've done everything you can. At some point, you do have to let any remaining fear be your compass and go for it. You've planned and prepared and have the skills you need to be successful.

Whatever happens next after you leap "is what it is." You have everything you need to succeed, repair, or pivot and win, so just let go and enjoy who you become in the process! Any successful entrepreneur will tell you that making that *one* decision to finally "go for it" was the best decision they've ever made.

23 I learned this from Bedros Keulian in his book, *Man Up*.

➢ We Can Be Our Own Worst Enemy

One of my favorite songs is by Andy Mineo and is called "You Can't Stop Me." In it, he goes through all the things his "opponent" does to try and stop him, every negative thing he says, all that he sees and points out, and so on: *"You're my biggest opponent...Whenever I fail you've always been there to simply remind me I've blown it...You know my mistakes, you never let it go...you catch every detail that I miss..."*

He then goes on to say, *"...if you know who I'm talkin' about, then you got me. My biggest enemy is me, and even I can't stop me."* I love that, not only because of the ending ("even I can't stop me") but also because of how true it is. We are often our biggest critic and the one that casts the most doubt on our abilities to succeed.

I know for me personally, being my own worst enemy is a defense mechanism of sorts: "As long as I criticize myself and find all my faults and the reasons I'll fail, then no one else can do it." Whatever the reason we beat ourselves up - often in advance of even trying - we can overcome it.

Start by taking some time to recognize what you've accomplished already in life. Write down your past "wins," however big or small. Remember all the times you've taken a risk in business and succeeded (even as an employee). While you're at it, record a few of the scenarios where you "failed" but still went on to succeed after you pivoted or changed direction. Then flip back through all of the work you've done through this process of building a new business and see what you've accomplished so far.

It's easy to catch our faults - they stand out in our own minds. But it's a lot more fruitful and confidence inspiring to see how many times we've won over our lifetimes. And, since we've won so much, what's to make us think we can't do it again? We've survived everything thus far and we're alive and ready to fight another day. We've got whatever comes next, and this "victory log" will keep that front of mind.[24]

➢ Others Mean Well (Usually)

Whether we're our own worst enemy or not at times, it can seem the people rooting against us the most are those closest to us. I believe that these people aren't criticizing and second guessing intentionally. Sometimes they even think they're trying to help. You can't control what others say, but you can control your exposure to them and how you let it affect your mind.

Other people can cause us to stop taking action in one of two ways. First is our own concern about what others think about us. Usually, this has more to do with strangers or clients or random people, but it can also come from our families. We simply can't let *what we think others are thinking about us* influence our decisions about our own futures.

Ed Mylett said it best: "Don't worry about what other people are thinking about you. They are too busy wondering what you're thinking about them to think about you!"

The reality is that even if you do "fail," two things are likely to happen: (1) you pivot one or more times and become successful (since that's what's always happened so far!), and (2) the person whose opinion you were worrying about probably forgot about you 30 seconds later. *Worry about what you, your Family of Choice, and God (if you believe in Him) think about you and forget everyone else's opinion.* Once you win, you won't have to worry about it again.

---

24 I first heard of the concept of a "victory log" from a Zig Ziglar book from the 1970s. I'd encourage you to create one and add to it with all of the wins - big and small - that you experience.

Second, those closest to us can try and talk us out of big decisions in order to "protect us." They mean well (usually) and don't want us to get "hurt" or see us "suffer," *especially* those who have been content to have a "good, steady job" for many years - or even their whole lives. What they're missing is the hurt and suffering you probably feel now, stuck in your job and not living out your potential. They don't understand the burning need you have to be your own boss and control your future. Remember, not everyone is called to be self-employed.

The best strategy I've seen for dealing with this came from Bedros Keullian in his book *Man Up*. He said to tell these people you need 90 days. If, at the end of that 90 days you're not making progress, you'll hear them out. Until then, you need their unconditional support. Odds are, that'll be enough to show you're serious and you might even be surprised at the support and belief they show (because they know you really believe it).

➢ What's Different This Time

Perhaps you've had struggles taking action before. If so, welcome to the club! Every successful person has. What makes those individuals come out on top (instead of staying down) is that they took action on the *next* thing. Most of the time, they learned something from the "false starts" or "failures" and go on to apply it to what's next. One of my mentors is known for saying, "I've failed more times than anyone I know, and *that* is why I succeed.[25]"

What you've been working on, this new venture of yours, *that is what's next for you*. You've planned your business, tested your offer, built up a financial runway, and are clear on who you will serve and

25 Shane Rudman, the author of *God Wants YOU to Win!*

how you will do it. You have what you need. *You are what you need. You are the prize.* That's what's different this time!

➢ How To Make Taking Action Easier (And Even Enjoyable)

When I think about the balance between fear and action when it comes to moving forward with a plan to launch, I think about those old fashion scales where you'd put weights on each side to balance it out. If you had too much weight on one end, the scale would tilt in that direction.

I believe our ability to take action is a lot like that. When we first get ready to launch, we may have a lot of "fear weight" holding down the "no go" end. As we overcome some of those fears, the weight decreases and, if we add enough inspiration, planning, expertise, and confidence to the other side, we can tip the scales in our favor and launch into action.

That motivation can come from different sources, not the least of which is going back to your "why," core values, mission statement, and what is driving you to self-employment in the first place. A lot of times a simple reminder from those areas will do the trick, especially if you repeat it over and over. Sometimes, we need a little more of a "nudge" to get going and take action. To make this easier, consider a few different options that can tip the scales in your favor.

Create A "Cornerstone"

Historically, a cornerstone is the first stone or block that was put in a new building, pyramid, or other structure. It signified the beginning of something new and exciting that brought value to many. In the context of launching a business, a "cornerstone" can serve as a regular reminder of what you stand to gain in making the leap.

There's a great story of how Jim Carrey, the actor, wrote himself a $10 million check and carried it around in his wallet as a reminder that he would hit it big and get paid that amount for a movie at some point. He eventually earned that amount for *Ace Ventura*. The check was a "cornerstone" for the actor and served as a constant reminder of what he was capable of and his goal.

What object could you set on your desk, carry around, or have show up on your phone at regular intervals to remind you of all you stand to gain as you make this move? It could be a picture of your kids, something you really want, a sign that says "Freedom," a poker chip, coin, or mug with an impactful message on it, etc. Get creative and find (or make) something that will constantly be in front of you and keep you focused and motivated on the big picture.

Enlist Help, But Be Careful

When you launch your business and go out on your own, it's easy to feel like you're on an island. One of the most freeing things you'll experience is discovering that there are others like you, both where you are now and those with businesses already successfully launched.

Seeking out these groups and people does two things for you. First, it reframes your view on success because you see dozens (or hundreds) of others who have achieved what you're working toward. Second, you're able to spend time with peers that can help you make decisions, take action, and even be potential referral partners.

Not only can being around the right people build your confidence and accelerate your journey, but it helps to offset any negativity you might get from others (or even from your own mind sometimes). Then, when you're successful, you get to pay it forward and return the favor. It's a win-win.

In the resource section (breakfreemoneybook.com/resources) I've included a list of the programs, groups, and masterminds I'm currently part of and the ones I've found to be the best resources not only for the above, but for potential clients and partners. Things always change, so I plan to keep this list updated for you.

Visualize Walking Through And Your Success

A few years back I had a military and airline pilot friend teach me about what he calls "chair flying." Essentially, pilots will sit in a chair, close their eyes, and "fly" through an entire mission, seeing every step of the way and each action they take before they get ready to take off and go. He shared with me that, while it might sound odd at first, it allows pilots to see their success first in their heads, creating confidence and a form of muscle memory for when they fly the real mission.

Slowly but surely, I started to apply "chair flying" and visualizing successfully taking action in my own life. I found that closing my eyes and seeing myself take the first few actions of launching my business helped me "feel" the wins and build confidence that it *is* doable. I have a business coach that always repeats the phrase, "Before you can go there in your body, you have to go there in your mind."[26]

In other words, visualizing can be a powerful tool to prepare you for what's to come and, ultimately, success. There are plenty of stories

---

[26] This is a core component in Micheal Burt's "Monster Producer" program.

of basketball teams splitting into two groups: those that visualized free throws before shooting and those that didn't. Even controlled for all variables, the ones that visualized tended to make significantly more baskets.

Create or find a cornerstone to keep fresh in your mind what you stand to gain from your successful move to self-employment. Position yourself around the right people in the same situation as - and even ahead of - you. Visualize your action steps and success. If you do these things, I believe you'll be surprised how easily taking the leap (and winning) come together!

➢ Summarizing Taking Action And Your Big Decision Point

Taking action is the key to success. That's the one step that's left to launch and take control of your future. Use the tools above to overcome fear and doubt and balance your scales with the techniques to make executing easier. That is all that's left!

Now, you're at a decision point.

You've done everything you can to stack the deck in your favor. *Millions* have gone before you successfully, many with far less certainty and planning than you have now.

In front of you are two paths. Path one - you can remain doing what you're doing and not take the leap, wondering all along if you could have (and even knowing that you probably would have) succeeded.

Path two - you take what you've built through this process and simply *go*. You execute. You take action and charge forward. *This* is the path that sets you free; the one that shows your kids and family what's possible and that gives you total control over your future and your destiny.

If you choose path two, take the leap and welcome yourself to *total freedom!*

CONCLUSION

Here you are!

Congratulations for making it through this process. You've taken an inventory of your skills, identified what you can uniquely do to launch your own business, put all the pieces together, formalized it, and are building your financial runway.

You have everything you need to be successful and make the move to self-employment. Put your plan together, schedule your tasks, and get to work! Feed your mind the right information and keep the negativity far away and I believe you'll "wake up" a few months from now in an exciting spot, far ahead of where you are now.

I've used this process multiple times and have seen it work for many clients, too. It is my hope that this structure is the key for you to accomplish great things and be in control of your future.

Nothing here is new, and very (very) little is unique to me. It's a combination of principles and strategies that have been around for a long time. That means they work! They have been proven. Take confidence in that as you begin your journey.

Thank you for taking the time to read this book and work through implementing the tasks. It means the world to me and I can't wait to see you succeed!

PS - This is just the beginning, and please make sure to join the Break Free Email Community for some great additional resources and connections at:

BreakFreeMoneyBook.com/EmailFamily

I'm rooting for you, because the more of us that reach true freedom, the more we can inspire others to do the same!

BONUS

How To Determine How Much Money You Need To Live The Life You Want

A natural question when you first look to break free is, "How will I replace my salary?" If you're making a multi-six-figure income now, it can be daunting to think about getting back to where you are now or "starting over." The good news is the amount you really need to live the life you want is usually lower than what you're earning now. Not always, but usually.

This means that taking the time to figure out how much it costs each month - and over the long-term - to run your life can save you quite a bit of stress in establishing your financial runway and self-employed income targets.

This section will give you an idea of what you need to have coming in each month now, plus what you might need in the future, to live the life you want. Think of it as a "mini financial plan" for your cash flow and long-term net worth.

➢ Determining How Much You Need To Earn To Live The Life You Want

There are five steps I use in my own life and with clients to figure out exactly how much income is needed to fund a particular lifestyle on a monthly basis. The effort is worth the reward, and it's possible this may be the most clarity you've had on your financial life to date.

Those steps are:

1. Figure out what you *really* want to do and experience
2. Calculate how much each of those items costs on a monthly basis (whether they are long-term or regularly occurring)
3. Estimate how much you'll need to earn, accounting for taxes
4. Establish that number as your monthly goal
5. Map out a plan to generate the income required to get there

This is one time where doing the math by hand can actually be helpful as it will ingrain some of the numbers into your head. That being said, I don't make clients do it, so I won't do that to you, either! There is a helpful spreadsheet to do the math for you on the resource site (breakfreemoneybook.com/resources).

You're a few minutes away from having a clear picture of what you need to earn now and as life goes on to reach your financial goals. Let's get started!

➢ Step 1 - Determine What You Really Want To Have Available

What do you want your life to look like as you make the transition to self-employment? What do you really *need* to be happy and live the life you want? You're always better off going through life with a clear target of what you want, knowing that all of the work you put in is designed to get you there.

Start by listing out what it is you really want to do. You're not worried about the *costs*, yet. Only identifying the places, people, things, etc. that make up your ideal life. We'll add the cost component next (and follow-up with what that means to you long-term and from an income standpoint later).

Here are some questions to get you thinking.

Where do you want to live? What type of home do you want? What's around it and where is it located, specifically?

What kind of hobbies and activities do you want to do? Are there places you want to travel, and if so, how often? What are your favorite things to do with friends and family that you want to continue or expand?

Who do you want to spend time with? What family and friends are important to you and who do you want to make sure you can afford to do things with (or for), and are there any people you want to make sure you can support financially?

If you have kids, what do you want for them? Is it paying for education, having funds to support them starting their own business, or do you want to make sure they can experience adventures and travel? What about private school or other near-term desires?

What kind of "things" do you want? What cars do you want to drive, if they are important to you? Do you like to have the latest clothes, appliances, etc.?

How do you want to spend your everyday time? Do you want to eat out regularly, or are you more interested in cooking with the family? Do you play a lot of golf or cycle and want to support that activity? What is important to you aside from work that you want to account for?

Do you like to invest in education, growth, and coaching for yourself? What type of training and masterminds do you want to invest in each month (or year)?

Everyone is different, so what works for others doesn't have to work for you. This exercise is another area to bring your family (or Family of Choice) in on to make sure everyone is on the same page.

There's no need to focus on expanding your lifestyle with these exercises, either. For many people, it's about cutting down to the *things that really matter.* As you transition to self-employed, you may find that a lot of your spending and activities were more of a "I worked hard for this so I might as well enjoy it" expense and not something truly meaningful to you.

You may find that you don't need as much as you're making now to live a meaningful life. Move on to the next step when you feel confident about your list.

➢ Step 2 - Calculate The Monthly Cost Of Each Of Your Meaningful Lifestyle Items

Don't shortchange the last part of Step 1. Make sure you go through your list of things you really want to do and identify the ones that truly matter and impact your happiness and fulfillment. Everything costs money and prioritizing pays off here.

You want to assign a dollar amount to each item on your list that represents its monthly cost. Not everything will work out as an even monthly number. Some expenses will have yearly numbers (such as travel) and others may be a single payment (or series of payments) at some point in time (such as education for your kids, a boat, etc.). Let's walk through how to calculate each of those.

Consistent Monthly Expenses

The easiest expenses to calculate are those that you spend roughly the same amount on monthly. These could include eating out, groceries, private school tuition, insurance, utilities, and so on.

Even though some vary each month (think of your electric or gas bill), there's a good chance you have an average you can rely on here. For those expenses, write the monthly cost next to each.

Break down each of your irregular expenses (the ones that may be annual or "lumpy" throughout the year) into monthly numbers. The easiest place to start are the bigger annual expenses you have.

Bigger Annual Expense Items

Some expenses like annual family trips, holidays, home maintenance, and so on don't fit nicely into monthly numbers. When that occurs, you want to add up the total cost on a yearly basis for each item.

To turn these yearly expenses into a monthly figure, simply calculate what you spend each year and divide by 12 (since there are 12 months in the year).

Calculate the average monthly number for each of those expenses and add them to your list next to the respective item. Next, focus on the one-time or one-off expenses and convert those to monthly numbers.

One-Off And One-Time Expense Items

There are two ways you can consider calculating how much you need for "one-off" or "one-time" items.

First, you can determine how much each will cost and the associated monthly payment. This method works best for things like purchasing a home (or additional home) or other assets that you expect to own for a long period of time. Alternatively, you can determine how much it will cost as a single payment in the future and then earmark savings to reach that goal. Read on to learn more about each

Determining The Monthly Payment Amount

If you have a big purchase in mind, such as a home, you can figure out the cost of owning that home by the monthly payment required. Borrowing money - and using this approach - allows you to access your purchase sooner. You will also pay it off in the future, which means that monthly cost drops.

The easiest way to arrive at the monthly number is to search for "monthly payment calculator." You'll find a number of them, and at the time of this writing, Bankrate.com has a workable option. (Just don't click the credit card or loan offers next to it!)

For any of the online calculators, you need to know the total cost of what you plan to borrow (usually the purchase price minus anything you put down), how long you will have the loan (called the "term"), and what the interest rate will be.

The term for the loan is based on what you are purchasing, but a good, quick guideline is 30 years for a home and five years for a vehicle. For other items you can choose a timeframe that you feel fits. For the interest rate, most calculators will have something built in that can give you an idea of the rate. If there isn't anything already there, you can pick a flat percentage, such as 5%, 7%, or similar to start.

(These are simple examples to get you started, not advice. There are plenty of options and opinions on the above, but the goal of this bonus section is to help you quickly add up what you need to live the life you want with your new business).

The output from the calculator gives you the monthly cost of ownership of the item in question, so go ahead and put that down in the appropriate area on your working chart.

Planning To Save Money To Purchase Directly

If you don't plan to finance or borrow for the purchase of the one-off or big, one-time items, saving funds ahead of time is an excellent strategy. The math works similarly in that you need to determine the total price of the item and how long you have until you acquire it.

(If there is a longer period of time before you look to purchase whatever it is you're considering, such as seven years or more, you may consider investing the money to help it grow. This isn't guaranteed, and is beyond the scope of this bonus section, but it should help the bottom line by reducing the amount you would need to save because you'd be earning a return on the dollars you put aside. As before, this is just for educational purposes and is not specific financial advice for you or any one individual.)

The simplest way to do this is to take the purchase price and divide it by the number of months you have until you acquire it. For example, if you want something that's $50,000 in five years, we multiply five x 12 to get the number of months (60 months in this case). Then, we divide $50,000 by 60 and get $833.33 a month. That would be the figure you'd need to save monthly, based on the time frame and desired amount. Place that in the appropriate area on your list.

Of course, many people will combine borrowing money and making a down payment.

A quick note: if you're finding that these expenses are adding up quickly, this is a good time to revisit which of these items really mean the most to you in the near term (Step 1). When you do that, you might discover a lot of the things you've listed are "wants" and not "needs" when it comes to your happiness and fulfillment.

As time goes on and your business and income grows, you can add a lot of these "bigger" or "extra" items back in. I'd encourage you to focus on the lifestyle items that really move the needle for you and your family for now, though. That will make the journey to self-employed - and hitting your income targets - much smoother.

➢ Step 3 - Estimate How Much You'll Need To Earn And Account For Taxes

Now that you have an idea of the monthly cost to live the life you want, you can work backward to determine the amount of income you need to earn on a monthly basis. It's a simple process that will tell you what you need to target to cover all of your expenses (and still save some for the future).

Let's use an example to illustrate the math. Let's say that, in Step 2, you determined that you would need $10,000 a month to live the life you want.

Your first instinct may be, "OK, I need to earn $10,000 a month then!" That's close, but you also need to account for taxes and any extra expenses that may result from being self-employed (such as health insurance).

Taxes are complex, but there are some good guidelines you can use to estimate closely enough to the amount of income you need to generate, taking taxes into consideration. Before we estimate those figures, know that this isn't specific tax or financial advice for you. It is for illustrative purposes only and you should consult a tax or financial advisor for your specific situation.

With that said, current and historic tax rates have been between 0% and 40% in recent times. Add in a self-employment and payroll tax of around 15%[27] and you could be anywhere from 15% to 65% as a self-employed individual for federal (IRS) taxes. If your state has an additional income tax rate, you can add this to the percentage.

Before you get too concerned about the taxes, know that you're likely already paying them as an employee! Sure, you will probably have slightly higher tax rates as a self-employed person due to the "employer" part of payroll taxes, but you will also likely have far more deductions available to you, too. These deductions can reduce your income tax bill.

I have found that most people don't experience a significant *net* increase in taxes simply as a result of becoming self-employed. The additional deductions tend to offset the additional tax burden, but you'll want to get a good idea of your own figures.

---

[27] At the time of this writing (2022), this is broken down to 15.3%, with part of it being Social Security and the other Medicare. There is a range around $147k that changes each year where the portion dedicated to Social Security stops. Again, please consult your tax advisor.

Here are a few rough-estimate guidelines:

If you are earning under $10,000 a month, you should be safe estimating a total federal tax impact of 30%.

Between $10,000 and $25,000 a month, you could use an estimate of 35%.

And above $25,000 a month, you can use an estimate of around 40%.

What does this mean for you as you calculate your needs? Using the example above of needing $10,000 a month to live the life you want, you know you will need to earn between $10,000 and $25,000 a month in income. That means we can use an estimated tax rate of 35%.

There are two steps to calculate the tax impact.

First, subtract your tax percentage from the number "1." For example, if you will use 35% for your tax bracket, you will do this math: 1 - 0.35 to give you 0.65.

Second, you take your monthly need of $10,000 and divide it by 0.65 ($10,000 / 0.65). This gives you $15,385 a month of income needed to generate $10,000 a month *after-tax*.

It's simple but messy (welcome to the tax code!). Keep in mind all you're doing is subtracting your tax rate from 1 and then dividing your monthly expense dollar amount by that number.

You may feel the number is high or low, but either way, you now know what your target is!

➢ Step 4 - Establish Your Monthly Goal Number

Knowing your target income from Step 3 gives you the ability to establish your "monthly goal number." This is the amount you need to earn to live the life you want.

It may be more or less than your current salary. Either way, your objective now is to figure out what actions you should take to earn that amount of money.

Continuing the example above where you want $10,000 a month after-tax (meaning you need to earn $15,385 before-tax), you can ask, "What do I need to do to generate $15,385 a month in income?"

You may have the answers already (that's what the previous chapters around building your business are designed to help you figure out) or you may still be seeking those out. If you're still looking, go back through Part 1 of the book and determine what you can do to generate income through your own business.

➢ Step 5 - Map Out Your Plan To Generate The Income Required

Once you're aware of your monthly goal number and are building your action plan to get there, all that's left is taking action!

Map out the specific plan you'll use to generate that income with your new business and get to work. It really is that simple, and that's the key to breaking free successfully!

You may find that you don't need as much income as you thought to live the life you want. That can be exciting as it makes your break-free goal that much more attainable.

Time to get to work!

DON'T MISS THESE FREE TOOLS!

BreakFreeMoneyBook.com/Resources

Here you will get free access to several worksheets and "extras" to help you safely and smartly make the move to self-employment!

You'll also have the opportunity to join our free community for support and even win some one-on-one coaching to help you break free!

BreakFreeMoneyBook.com/Resources

ABOUT THE AUTHOR

Andy Garrison brings a deep passion for entrepreneurship to his wealth management practice, continually working to be the absolute best at what he does. He credits his grandfather for sparking his lifelong journey of striving for for excellence, a quest that continues to fuel his professional growth.

As the author of *Million-Air*, a practical guide for airline pilots on wealth management, Andy has a knack for making complex financial concepts accessible to people with a host of various economic concerns and needs. In addition to his book, he contributes his insights to numerous blogs and articles and enjoys being a guest on various industry-related podcasts.

Andy's commitment extends beyond the financial world, with his faith and family standing as pillars for his life. He finds joy in helping others to achieve financial independence and professional freedom.

Andy enjoys spending time with his family (both two, and four-legged), and lives in the Kansas City area.

ACKNOWLEDGMENTS

The list is long of those who have helped me learn the lessons that allowed me to break free successfully and, as a follow up, share that process with the world through this book.

Above all, my journey started with a prompting from God to take this journey and make it into something that could help others. Without the vision He shared with me of "mastering the move to self-employment and bringing 100 others with me," I never would have gotten started. There is no better guide than You, Lord.

To my two kids, "E" and "C." You two inspired me to reach for me and do my small part to show you what's possible. You are my drive to be the best I can be. My hope is that, one day, this book becomes a resource that leads you to whatever journey you choose with confidence.

To my wife, Erin, for always being by my side and giving me clear and concise guidance through this process. Without you, this wouldn't have happened (and our life would be nowhere near where it is now).

To Shane Rudman for opening up my eyes to what's possible and new levels of accomplishment, all while helping me keep my eyes focused on Him and what matters most. Your lessons and teachings have helped thousands, and I am forever grateful for the time you shared with me on this path.

To my late Grandpa Garrison, still the most amazing man I know. We shared many good conversations and memories, and the lessons you taught stick with me to this day. Not only did you share, but you showed the true meaning of love and real success. You are my beacon of what I hope to be as an entrepreneur, and I smile every time I think of you chatting with some of the best up there.

To my parents, who stuck with me through thick and thin and remain by my side to this day. No matter how many ideas I've had or attempts I've made, you've had my back and showed me what unconditional support really is.

To Jack Giardino, who will accomplish incredible things in this world. Not only have you proven to be the ideal partner in business, but your assistance in getting some of the tools together for this book was critical in making it valuable and helpful.

To all of those who have poured into me through books, podcasts, courses, and mentorship, thank you. You have done more for me and my family than I can ever repay. My hope is this book, to a small degree, carries forward your movements. There are too many to name, but I'd be remiss if I didn't thank Nick Koumalatsos, Micheal Burt, Drewbie Wilson, and, once again, Shane Rudman. I owe so much to each of you.

Finally, thank you to YOU, the reader! If this book can help just one of you create freedom for yourself and your family, you have done more for me than I could even share.

Made in the USA
Monee, IL
04 November 2026

67380038R00128